Reading Women's Lives
AN INTRODUCTION TO WOMEN'S STUDIES

COMPILED BY
INSTRUCTOR (YOUR NAME HERE)

(SCHOOL NAME)
(COURSE NAME AND NUMBER)

SIMON & SCHUSTER CUSTOM PUBLISHING

Cover Art: *The Very Rich Hours: From the Land of the Silk Dragon,* by Joanne Stichweh, 1992.

Printed in the United States of America

10 9 8 7 6 5 4 3 2 1

ISBN 0–536–00232–0

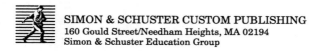 SIMON & SCHUSTER CUSTOM PUBLISHING
160 Gould Street/Needham Heights, MA 02194
Simon & Schuster Education Group

Contributors

Editor
Mary Margaret Fonow

Managing Editor
Lucy Bailey

Editorial Board
Elizabeth Allan
Nancy D. Campbell
Susan M. Hartmann
Sally L. Kitch
Judith Mayne
Martha L. Wharton

Contributing Editors

Elizabeth Allan	Education
Linda Bernhard	Health and Medicine
Carol Bohmer	Law and Legal Theory
Nancy D. Campbell	Family Relations
	Politics, Government and Policy
	Science, Gender and Technology
Ron Eglash	Science, Gender and Technology
Mary Margaret Fonow	Difference and Inequality
	Work, Poverty and Economic Policy
Leigh Gilmore	Autobiography (Co-editor 1996-97)
Susan M. Hartmann	Feminism and Women's Movements
Sally L. Kitch	Motherhood and Reproduction
Valerie Lee	The Body
Judith Mayne	Women, Representation and Culture
Birch Moonwomon-Baird	Language
Ara Wilson	Sexualities
Martha L. Wharton	Religion
Ara Wilson	International Perspectives
Adriane Livingston	International Perspectives
Willa Young	Violence

Article Introductions and Discussion Questions
Lucy Bailey
Lin Distel

An example of a custom book from the Simon & Schuster database of material on women's studies

Reading Women's Lives is an on-demand database publishing program consisting of a wide variety of material on women's studies. The articles and readings included in this database were selected by the Department of Women's Studies at The Ohio State University. Choose only the material you want to use from the comprehensive master list to create a quality book customized to fit your curriculum. See pages vii–xxix for a current listing of available articles and readings.

Features of a custom book using the *Reading Women's Lives* database

- Total flexibility and customization. Choose from over 300 articles and readings to create a book that matches your teaching style.

- Freedom to include your own material. Contact Simon & Schuster Custom Publishing for guidelines on how to submit your original material for inclusion in your custom reader.

- Worry-free permissions—Simon & Schuster Custom Publishing handles all associated copyright clearances.

- Custom title page including the instructor's name, school, and course name and number.

- A standard design throughout the book for all materials from the *Reading Women's Lives* database.

- High quality, professional printing and sequential pagination throughout the entire book.

- Fast and economical—only 3–4 weeks to complete an initial order—minimum order of 25 copies.

- Personalized, toll-free customer service—call 1-800-428-4466.

Ordering and pricing a custom book using the *Reading Women's Lives* database

For more information or to request an order form please contact us at:

Simon & Schuster Custom Publishing
Reading Women's Lives database
160 Gould Street
Needham, MA 02194

TEL: 800-428-4466

FAX: 781-455-1707

e-mail: Women's_Studies@Prenhall.com

Visit our web site at:

www.sscp.com/womens_studies

Pricing: The cost of the reader depends on the total number of pages included. There is a base price of $5.00 and $0.07/per page. Generally, readers that are approximately 200 pages are less than $20.00 to the student. The final price is determined by the bookstore.

Autobiography

By Leigh Gilmore

Angelou, Maya. From *I Know Why the Caged Bird Sings*. (1969)

Anzaldúa, Gloria. "La Conciencia de la mestiza: Towards a New Consciousness." *Borderlands/ La Frontera: The New Mestiza*. (1987)

Cheng, Nien. From *Life and Death in Shanghai*. (1986)

Conway, Jill Ker. "Drought." *The Road from Coorain*. (1989)

Hayslip, Le Ly. From *When Heaven and Earth Changed Places*. (1989)

Hong-Kingston, Maxine. "No Name Woman." *The Woman Warrior*. (1977)

Kincaid, Jamaica. From *A Small Place*. (1988)

Lorde, Audre. From *Zami: A New Spelling of My Name*. (1982)

Stein, Gertrude. From *The Autobiography of Alice B. Toklas*. (1933)

Suleri, Sara. "Meatless Days." *Meatless Days*. (1989)

The Body

By Valerie Lee

Aldrich, Marcia. "Hair." *Northwest Review*. (1992)

Allison, Dorothy. "From *Two or Three Things I Know for Sure*." (1995)

Bynum, Caroline Walker. "The Female Body and Religious Practice in the Later Middle Ages." *Fragmentation and Redemption: Essays on Gender and the Human Body in Medieval Redemption*. (1991)

Cahn, Susan K. "From the 'Muscle Moll' to the 'Butch' Ballplayer: 'Mannishness,' Lesbianism, and and Homophobia in U.S. Women's Sports." *Feminist Studies.* (1992)

Changing Norms of Beauty. *Godey's Lady's Book and Harper's Bazaar.* (1848/1908)

Cowley, Geoffrey. "The Biology of Beauty." *Newsweek.* (1996)

Dykstra, Jean. "Putting Herself in the Picture: Autobiographical Images of Illness and the Body." *Afterimage.* (1995)

Frueh, Joanna. "The Body Through Women's Eyes." *The Power of Feminist Art: The American Movement of the 1970s, History and Impact.* (1994)

Grant, Stephanie. "Posting Up." *Agog.* (1990)

Grealy, Lucy. "Mirrorings: To Gaze Upon My Reconstructed Face." *Harper's.* (1993)

Hurston, Zora Neale. "From *Their Eyes Were Watching God.*" (1978)

Mairs, Nancy. "Carnal Acts." *Carnal Acts.* (1990)

Moraga, Cherríe. "From *Loving in the War Years.*" (1983)

Difference and Inequality

By Mary Margaret Fonow

Anzaldúa, Gloria. "La Conciencia de la mestiza: Towards a New Consciousness." *Borderlands/ La Frontera: The New Mestiza.* (1987)

Baca Zinn, Maxine and Bonnie Thornton Dill. "Theorizing Difference from Multiracial Feminism." *Feminist Studies.* (1996)

Bunch, Charlotte. "Making Common Cause: Diversity and Coalitions." *Passionate Politics: Essays 1968-1986.* (1987)

Childress, Alice. "The Pocketbook Game." (1956)

Chrystos. "I am Not Your Princess." *Not Vanishing.* (1988)

Cofer, Judith Ortiz. "The Myth of the Latin Woman: I Just Met a Girl Named Maria." *The Latin Deli.* (1993)

duCille, Ann. "Dyes and Dolls: Multicultural Barbie and the Merchandizing of Difference." *Differences: A Journal of Women's Cultural Studies.* (1994)

Frye, Marilyn. "Oppression." *The Politics of Reality: Essays in Feminist Theory.* (1983)

Gould, Louis. "X: A Fabulous Child's Story." *Ms. (1972)*

King, Ynestra. "The Other Body: Reflections on Difference, Disability, and Identity Politics." *Ms.* (1993)

Lorde, Audre. "Age, Race, Class and Sex: Women Redefining Difference." *Sister Outsider.* (1984)

Pharr, Suzanne. Excerpt from "Homophobia: A Weapon of Sexism." (1988)

Steinem, Gloria. "Rebecca Adamson." *Ms.* (1997)

Thompson, Becky. "Time Traveling and Border Crossing: Reflections on White Identity." *Names We Call Home: Autobiography on Racial Identity.* (1996)

Villarosa, Linda. "Coming Out." *Essence.* (1991)

Wernick, Laura. "Jewish and White: Issues of Passing." *The Present Generation: Issues on College Campuses (Panel Discussion).* (1990)

Williams, Patricia. "Hate Radio: Why We Need to Tune into Limbaugh and Stern." *Ms.* (1994)

Willie, Sarah. "Playing the Devil's Advocate: Defending a Multiracial Identity in Fractured Community." *Names We Call Home: Autobiography on Racial Identity.* (1996)

Woo, Deborah. "The Gap Between Striving and Achieving: The Case of Asian-American Women." *Making Waves: An Anthology of Writings By and About Asian Women.* (1989)

Yamato, Gloria. "Something About the Subject Makes It Hard to Name." *Changing Our Power.* (1988)

Education

By Elizabeth Allan

Bell, Lee Ann. "Something Is Wrong Here and It's Not Me: Challenging the Dilemmas that Block Girls' Success." *Journal for the Education of the Gifted.* (1989)

Berkow, Ira. "Walking Away, While He Still Can." *The New York Times.* (1993)

Blais, Madelaine. "In these Girls, Hope is a Muscle." *The New York Times Magazine.* (1993)

Blum, Debra E. "College Sports L-Word." *The Chronicle of Higher Education.* (1994)

Christian, Barbara. "Camouflaging Race and Gender." *Representations.* (1996)

Clarke, Edward H. "Sex in Education." *Sex in Education: or, A Fair Chance for the Girls.* (1873)

Conway, M. Margaret, David Ahern and Gertrude Steuernagel. "Women and Educational Policy." *Women and Public Policy: A Revolution in Progress.* (1995)

Grant, Linda. "Helpers, Enforcers, and Go-Betweens: Black Females in Elementary School Classrooms." *Women of Color in U.S. Society.* (1994)

Holland, Dorothy, and Margaret Eisenhart. "Getting into the World of Romance and Attractiveness." *Educated in Romance: Women, Achievement and College Culture.* (1990)

LaDuke, Winona. "Nitzitapi and the Blackfeet Community." *Indigenous Woman.* (1996)

McNaghten, Marci. "A Sporting Chance for Women." *Ohio State Quest.* (1994)

Murray, Lori. "Left at the Starting Gate: Gender Inequality in Education." *Columbus Parent.* (1997)

Pollitt, Katha. "The Smurfette Principle." *The New York Times.* (1991)

Pollitt, Katha. "Why Boys Don't Play with Dolls." *The New York Times Magazine.* (1995)

Sadker, Myra and David. "Missing in Interaction." *Failing at Fairness: How America's Schools Cheat Girls.* (1994)

Sadker, Myra, David Sadker, Lynn Fox & Melinda Salata. "Gender Equity in the Classroom: The Unfinished Agenda." *College Board Review.* (1993)

Sittenfeld, Curtis. "Your Life as a Girl." *Listen Up!: Voices from the Next Feminist Generation.* (1995)

Tierney, William G. "Building Academic Communities of Difference: Gays, Lesbians, and Bisexuals on Campus." *Change.* (1992)

Thomas, M. Carey. "Present Tendencies in Women's College and University Education." *Educational Review.* (1908)

Family Relations

By Nancy D. Campbell

Allyn, Jennifer and David. "Identity Politics." *To Be Real.* (1995)

Baca Zinn, Maxine. "Family, Feminism and Race in America." *Race, Class and Gender: Common Bonds, Different Voices.* (1996)

Baca Zinn, Maxine. "Feminist Rethinking from Racial-Ethnic Families." *Women of Color in U.S. Society.* (1995)

Barnett, Rosalind and Caryl Rivers. "Look Who's Talking About Work and Family."*Ms.* (1996)

Browning, Frank. "Why Marry?" *New York Times.* (1996)

diLeonardo, Micaela. "The Female World of Cards and Holidays: Women, Families, and the Work of Kinship." *Signs.* (1987)

Hunter, Nan. "Sexual Dissent and the Family: The Sharon Kowalski Case." *The Nation.* (1991)

Lehrer, Susan. "Family and Women's Lives." *Women: Images and Realities—A Multicultural Anthology.* (1995)

May, Elaine Tyler. "Baby Boom and Birth Control." *Homeward Bound: American Families in the Cold War Era.* (1988)

Rauch, Jonathan. "For Better or Worse?" *New Republic.* (1996)

Stacey, Judith. "The Making and Unmaking of Modern Families." *Brave New Families.* (1991)

Syfers, Judy. "Why I Want a Wife." *Radical Feminism.* (1973)

Van Gelder, Lindsy. "Marriage as a Restricted Club." *Ms.* (1984)

Feminism and Women's Movements

By Susan M. Hartmann

Bunch, Charlotte. "Bringing the Global Home." *Passionate Politics: Essays 1968-1986.* (1987)

Chafe, William. "The Revival of Feminism." *The Paradox of Change: American Women in the 20ᵗʰ Century.* (1991)

Declaration of Sentiments and Resolutions, Seneca Falls. *Feminism: The Essential Historical Writings.* (1848)

DuBois, Ellen Carol. "The First Women's Rights Movement." *Feminism and Suffrage: The Emergence of an Independent Women's Movement in America 1848-1869.* (1978)

Echols, Alice. "Nothing Distant About It: Women's Liberation and Sixties Radicalism." *The Sixties: From Memory to History.* (1994)

Hogeland, Lisa Maria. "Fear of Feminism: Why Young Women Get the Willies." *Ms.* (1994)

hooks, bell. "Men in Feminist Struggle—The Necessary Movement." *Women Respond to the Men's Movement.* (1992)

Mansbridge, Jane. "What is the Feminist Movement?" *Feminist Organizations: Harvest of the New Women's Movement.* (1995)

Martinez, Elizabeth. "In Pursuit of Latina Liberation." *Signs.* (1995)

Neuborne, Ellen. "Imagine My Surprise." *Listen Up: Voices from the Next Feminist Generation.* (1995)

National Organization for Women. "NOW Statement of Purpose." *It Changed My Life: Writings on the Women's Movement.* (1966) and "NOW Bill of Rights." *Rebirth of Feminism.* (1968)

Painter, Nell. "Sojourner Truth's Defense of the Rights of Women." *Women's America: Refocusing the Past.* (1991)

Ruffin, Josephine St. Pierre. "Address to the First National Conference of Colored Women." *The Woman's Era by Josephine St. Pierre Ruffin.* (1895)

Sacks, Karen. "The Class Roots of Feminism." *Monthly Review.* (1976)

Smith, Barbara. "Introduction." *Home Girls: A Black Feminist Anthology.* (1983)

Truth, Sojourner. "Ain't I a Woman?" *Feminism: The Essential Historical Writings.* (1851)

Turner, Tracy Zollinger. "Feminism by Osmosis." *The Columbus Guardian.* (1994)

van der Gaag, Nikki. "Women: Still Something to Shout About." *New Internationalist.* (1995)

Wagner, Sally Roesch. "Is Equality Indigenous? The Untold Iroquois Influence on the Early Radical Feminists." *On the Issues: The Progressive Women's Quarterly.* (1996)

Walker, Alice. "Womanist." *In Search of Our Mothers' Gardens.* (1983)

Walker, Rebecca. "Becoming the Third Wave." *Ms.* (1992)

Wilson, Ara. "Lesbians Visibility and Sexual Rights at Beijing." *Signs.* (1996)

Health and Medicine

By Linda A. Bernhard

Bassuk, Ellen. "The Restcure: Repetition or Resolution of Victorian Women's Conflicts?" *The Female Body in Western Culture: Contemporary Perspectives*. (1986)

Chernik, Abra Fortune. "The Body Politic." *Listen Up!: Voices from the Next Feminist Generation*. (1995)

Crossette, Barbara. "New Tally of World Tragedy: Women Who Die Giving Life." *The New York Times*. (1996)

Delgado, Linda. "Arroz con Pollo vs. Slim Fast." *Women: Images and Realities—A Multicultural Reader*. (1995)

Doyal, Lesley. "Abusing Women." *What Makes Women Sick: Gender and the Political Economy of Health*. (1995)

Ehrenreich, Barbara and Deidre English. "The Doctors's Stake in Womens' Illness." "The Scientific Explanation of Female Frailty." *Complaints and Disorders: The Sexual Politics of Sickness*. (1973)

Ferraro, Susan. "You Can't Look Away Anymore: The Anguished Politics of Breast Cancer Activism." *The New York Times Magazine*. (1993)

Gorman, Christine. "Sizing up the Sexes." *Time*. (1992)

Goudsmit, Ellen M. "All in Her Mind! Stereotypic Views and the Psychologisation of Women's Illness." *Women & Health: Feminist Perspectives*. (1994)

Krieger, Nancy and Elizabeth Fee. "Man-Made Medicine and Women's Health: The Biopolitics of Sex/Gender and Race/Ethnicity." *Women's Health, Politics and Power: Essays on Sex/Gender, Medicine and Public Health*. (1994)

Martin, Emily. "Body Narratives, Body Boundaries." *Cultural Studies*. (1992)

Martin, Emily. "The Egg and the Sperm." *Signs*. (1991)

Ramsay, Heather. "Lesbians and the Health Care System: Invisibility, Isolation and Ignorance—You Say You're a What?" *Canadian Woman Studies.* (1994)

Thompson, Becky. "A Way Outa No Way: Eating Problems Among African American, Latina and White Women." *Race, Class and Gender.* (1996)

Valdés, Alisa L. "Ruminations of a Feminist Aerobics Instructor." *Listen Up!: Voices from the Next Feminist Generation.* (1995)

Villarosa, Linda, ed. "Introduction." *Body & Soul: The Black Women's Guide to Physical Health and Emotional Well-Being.* (1994)

International Perspectives

By Ara Wilson and Adriane Livingston

Bunch, Charlotte. "Transforming Human Rights from a Feminist Perspective. *Women's Rights, Human Rights: International Feminist Perspectives.* (1995)

Condé, Maryse. "Three Women in Manhattan." *Green Cane Juicy Flotsam: Short Stories by Caribbean Women.* (1991)

Copelon, Rhonda. "Gendered War Crimes: Reconceptualizing Rape in Time of War." *Women's Rights, Human Rights: International Feminist Perspectives.* (1995)

Dankelman, Irene and Joan Davidson. "Why Women?" *Women and Environment in the Third World.* (1988)

Enloe, Cynthia. "Gender Makes the World Go Round." *Bananas, Beaches & Bases: Making Feminist Sense of International Politics.* (1989)

Garcia-Moreno, Claudia. "AIDS: Women are Not Just Transmitters." *Changing Perceptions: Writings on Gender and Development.* (1991)

Hondagneu-Sotelo, Pierrette. "Women and Children First: New Directions in Anti-immigrant Politics." *Socialist Review.* (1995)

Hyvrard, Jeanne. "Opera Station. Six in the Evening. For Months . . ." *Green Cane Juicy Flotsam: Short Stories by Caribbean Women.* (1991)

Kristof, Nicholas. "Asian Childhoods Sacrificed to Prosperity's Lust." *The New York Times.* (1996)

Mayer, Ann Elizabeth. "Cultural Particularism as a Bar to Women's Rights: Reflections on the Middle Eastern Experience." *Women's Rights, Human Rights: International Feminist Perspectives.* (1995)

Menchú, Rigoberta. "Things Have Happened to Me as in a Movie." *You Can't Drown the Fire: Latin American Women Writing in Exile.* (1988)

National Council for Research on Women. "The Feminization of Immigration." *Issues Quarterly.* (1996)

Reagon, Bernice Johnson. "African Diaspora Women: The Making of Cultural Workers." *Women in Africa and the African Diaspora.* (1987)

Robertson, Claire. "Grassroots in Kenya: Women, Genital Mutilation, and Collective Action, 1920-1990." *Signs.* (1996)

Upton, Elaine Maria. "Born to the Struggle, Learning to Write: An Interview with Lindiwe Mabuza, Poet and Chief Representative of the African National Congress." *Feminist Studies.* (1995)

Wallace, Tina. "'Taking the Lion by the Whiskers': Building on the Strengths of the Refugee Women." *Changing Perceptions: Writings on Gender and Development.* (1991)

"Beyond Bejing." *Issues Quarterly.* (1996)

Language

By Birch Moonwomon-Baird

Cardall, Michelle Quinn. Can 'He' Mean 'She'? Exploring the Semantics of Political Correctness. *The Blair Reader.* (1994)

Eckert, Penelope and Sally McConnel-Ginet. "Think Practically and Look Locally: Language and Gender as Community-Based Practice." *Annual Review of Anthropology.* (1992)

Greenwood, Alice. "Children on Trial: Language Issues and Child Testimony." *Cultural Performances: Proceedings of the Third Berkeley Women and Language Conference.* (1994)

Hall, Kira. "A Third-Sex Subversion of a Two-Gender System." Unpublished paper. (1994)

Lorde, Audre. "The Transformation of Silence into Language and Action." *Sinister Wisdom.* (1978)

Mendoza-Denton, Norma. "Language Attitudes and Gang Affiliation Among California Latina Girls." *Cultural Performances: Proceedings of the Third Berkeley Women and Language Conference.* (1994)

Morgan, Marcyliena. "No Woman No Cry: The Linguistic Representation of African American Women." *Cultural Performances: Proceedings of the Third Berkeley Women and Language Conference.* (1994)

Nichols, Patricia. "Linguistic Options and Choices for Black Women in the Rural South." *Language, Gender and Society.* (1983)

Nilsen, Alleen Pace. "Sexism in English: A 1990s Update." *The Blair Reader.*

Sheldon, Amy. "Pickle Fights: Gendered Talk in Preschool Disputes." *The Feminist Critique of Language: A Reader.* (1993)

Tannen, Deborah. "The Relativity of Linguistic Strategies: Rethinking Power and Solidarity in Gender and Dominance." *Gender and Conversation Interaction.* (1993)

Thorne, Barrie, Cheris Kramarae, and Nancy Henely. "Language, Gender and Society: Opening the Second Decade of Research." *Language, Gender and Society.* (1983)

Law and Legal Theory

By Carol Bohmer

"Civil Rights Act, Title VII" (1964). *Women's America: Refocusing the Past.* (1995)

"Comstock Law" (1873). *Women's America: Refocusing the Past.* (1995)

"Declaration of Sentiments" (1848). *Feminism: The Essential Historical Writings.* (1992)

"Equal Rights Amendment" (1972). *Women's America: Refocusing the Past.* (1995)

"Equal Suffrage (Nineteenth) Amendment" (1920). *Women's America: Refocusing the Past.* (1995)

Glaspell, Susan. "A Jury of Her Peers." *Everyweek.* (1917)

Kessler, Alice-Harris. "Equal Employment Opportunity Commission vs. Sears, Roebuck and Company: A Personal Account." *Radical History Review.* (1986)

"The Law of Domestic Relations: Example from Colonial Connecticut, 1640-1702." *Women's America: Refocusing the Past.* (1995)

"Married Women's Property Acts, New York State, 1848, 1860." *Women's America: Refocusing the Past.* (1995)

"Meritor Savings Bank v. Mechelle Vinson et al., 1986." *Women's America: Refocusing the Past.* (1995)

"Roe v. Wade, 1973; Planned Parenthood of Southeastern Pennsylvania v. Casey, 1992." *Women's America: Refocusing the Past.* (1995)

Wellman, Judith. "The Seneca Falls Women's Rights Convention: A Study of Social Networks." *Journal of Women's History.* (1991)

Motherhood and Reproduction

By Sally L. Kitch

Allison, Dorothy. "Mama." *Trash.* (1988)

Anonymous. "African-American Women are For Reproductive Freedom." Conference Handout, Compliments of the National Black Woman's Self-Help Project, Atlanta, Georgia.

Chatterjee, Meera. "Creating Demand for Safe Motherhood." *Choices.*

Chira, Susan. "Study Says Babies in Child Care Keep Secure Bonds to Mothers." *The New York Times.* (1996)

Collins, Patricia Hill. "Black Women and Motherhood." *Black Feminist Thought: Knowledge, Consciousness, and the Politics of Empowerment.* (1991)

Daniels, Cynthia R. "Bodily Integrity and Forced Medical Treatment: The Case of Angela Carder." *At Women's Expense: State Power and the Politics of Fetal Rights.* (1993)

Davis, Angela. "Outcast Mothers and Surrogates: Racism and Reproductive Politics in the Nineties." *American Feminist Thought at Century's End: A Reader.* (1993)

Gilman, Charlotte Perkins. "The Unnatural Mother." *The Foreunner.* (1916)

Ginsburg, Faye. "From the Physician's Campaign to Roe vs. Wade." *Contested Lives.* (1989)

Grimké, Sarah. "Of Voluntary Motherhood." *Marriage, Weld Grimke Papers.* (1855)

Lewin, Ellen. "Natural Achievements: Lesbian Mothers in American Culture." *Lesbian Mothers: Accounts of Gender in American Culture.* (1993)

Regan, Donald H. "Statement of Prof. Donald Regan, School of Law, University of Michigan." *Congressional Hearings on the Constitutional Amendments Relating to Abortion.* (1981)

"Roe v. Wade." *Laws of Sex Discrimination.* (1988)

Sanger, Margaret. "Girl Mothers: Two," "Voices of the Children,Three & Six," "The Pinch of Poverty, Eighteen," "Conclusion." *Motherhood in Bondage.* (1928)

Usdansky, Margaret. "Single Motherhood: Stereotypes vs. Statistics." *The New York Times.* (1996)

Williams, Patricia. "The Unbearable Autonomy of Being." *The Rooster's Egg: On the Persistence of Prejudice.* (1995)

Politics, Government and Public Policy

By Nancy D. Campbell

Benokraitis Nijole and Joe Feagin. "Sex Discrimination in the 1990s: Progress and Illusions of Power." *Modern Sexism: Blatant, Subtle, and Covert Discrimination.* (1995)

Burstein, Karen and Lani Guinier. "What's Fair?" *Ms.* (1995)

Christian, Barbara. "Camouflaging Race and Gender." *Representations.* (1996)

Conway, M. Margaret, David W. Ahern and Gertrude Steuernagel. "Historical Background of Child Care and Family Leave Issues." *Women and Public Policy: A Revolution in Progess.* (1995)

Eason, Yla. "When the Boss Wants Sex." *Essence.* (1981)

Herttell, Thomas. "The Right Of Married Women to Hold and Control Property." *Against the Tide: Pro-Feminist Men in the United States 1776–1990.* (1839)

Hunter, Nan D. "Banned in the USA: What the Sodomy Ruling Will Mean." *The Village Voice.* (1986)

Kenny, Lorraine. "Affirming Diversity: Building a National Community That Works." "Points of Law." *Issues Quarterly.* (1996)

McLarin, Kimberly J. "Foor the Poor, Defining Who Deserves What." *The New York Times.* (1995)

McNaghten, Marci. "A Sporting Chance for Women." *Ohio State*

Quest. (1994)

Riordan, Teresa and Sue Kirchoff. "Women on the Hill: Can They Make a Difference?" *Ms.* (1995)

Schmitt, Eric. "War Is Hell. So Is Regulating Sex." *The New York Times.* (1996)

Woodman, Sue. "How Teen Pregnancy Has Become a Political Football." *Ms.* (1995)

Religion

By Martha L. Wharton

Bynum, Caroline Walker. "'. . . And Woman His Humanity': Female Imagery in the Religious Writing of the Later Middle Ages." *Fragmentation and Redemption: Essays on Gender and the Human Body in Medieval Redemption.* (1991)

Christ, Carol. P. "Why Women Need the Goddess: Phenomenological, Psychological, and Political Reflections." *Heresies.* (1982)

Grimké, Sarah. "Woman's Place in Religion: Nineteenth Century Views." *The Pastoral Letter of the General Association of Congregational Ministers of Massachusetts.* (1837)

Isasi-Díaz, Ada María and Yolanda Tarango. "Prologue." *Hispanic Women, Prophetic Voices in the Church.* (1992)

Kramer, Heinrich and James Sprenger. "The Malleus Maleficarum." (1971)

Lee, Jarena. "The Life and Religious Experience of Jarena Lee." *Sisters of the Spirit: Three Black Women's Autobiographies.* (1986)

Orenstein, Gloria Feman. "Toward an Ecofeminist Ethic of Shamanism and the Sacred." *Ecofeminism and the Sacred.* (1993)

Pagels, Elaine H. "What Became of God the Mother?: Conflicting Images of God in Early Christianity." *Signs.* (1976)

Plaskow, Judith. "Epilogue: The Coming of Lilith." *Womanspirit*

Rising: A Feminist Reader in Religion. (1979)

Plaskow, Judith. "The Coming of Lilith: Toward a Feminist Theology." *Womanspirit Rising: A Feminist Reader in Religion.* (1979)

Russell, Letty M. "Introduction." *The Liberating Word: A Guide to Nonsexist Interpretation of the Bible.* (1976)

Schaef, Anne Wilson. "Introduction." *Native Wisdom for White Minds.* (1995)

Stanton, Elizabeth Cady. "Introduction." *The Woman's Bible.* (1895)

Stewart, Maria. "Mrs. Stewart's Farewell Address to Her Friends in the City of Boston." (1833)

"The Trial of Anne Hutchinson." Excerpted from "Examination of Mrs. Anne Hutchinson before the court at Newton, 1637," *The Antinomian Controversy, 1636-1638: A Documentary History.*" (1637)

Trible, Phyllis. "Eve and Adam: Genesis 2-3 Reread." *Andover Newton Quarterly.* (1973)

Villarosa, Linda. "Revelations." *Essence.* (1995)

Williams, Delores S. "Womanist Theology: Black Women's Voices." *Weaving the Visions: New Patterns in Feminist Spirituality.* (1989)

Williams, Terry Tempest. "Burrowing Owls." *Refuge: An Unnatural History of Family and Place.* (1991)

Science, Gender and Technology

By Nancy D. Campbell and Ron Eglash

Barinaga, Marcia. "Is There a 'Female Style' in Science?" *Science.* (1993)

Barinaga, Marcia. "Feminists Find Gender Everywhere in Science." *Science.* (1993)

Cowley, Geoffrey. "The Biology of Beauty." *Newsweek.* (1996)

Hubbard, Ruth. "Rethinking Women's Biology." *The Politics of Women's Biology.* (1990)

Hubbard, Ruth. "Sexism in Sociobiology." *Profitable Promises.* (1995)

Keller, Evelyn Fox. "The Anomaly of a Woman in Physics." *Working It Out.* (1977)

Kolata, Gina. "Who Is Female: Science Can't Say." *New York Times.* (1992)

Sands, Aimee. "Never Meant to Survive (An Interview with Evelynn Hammonds)." *Radical Teacher.* (1986).

Turkle, Sherry. "Tinysex and Gender Trouble." *Life on the Screen.* (1995)

Sexualities

By Ara Wilson

Angier, Natalie. "Intersexual Healing: An Anomaly Finds a Group." *The New York Times.* (1996)

Anzaldúa, Gloria. "La Conciencia de la mestiza: Towards a New Consciousness." *Borderlands/ La Frontera: The New Mestiza.* (1987)

Bem, Ramazanoglu, Gill and Walker. "Heterosexual Feminist Identities." *Heterosexuality.* (1992)

Chalker, Rebecca. "Updating the Model of Female Sexuality." SIECUS Report. (1994)

Cott, Nancy F. "Passionless: An Interpretation of Victorian Sexual Ideology, 1790–1850." *Signs.* (1978)

Gomez, Jewell. "I Lost It At the Movies." *Testimonies: A Collection of Lesbian Coming Out Stories.* (1988)

Hammonds, Evelynn M. "Towards a Genealogy of Black Female Sexuality: The Problematic of Silence." *Feminist Genealogies, Colonial Legacies, Democratic Futures.* (1997)

Hollibaugh, Amber. "Desire for the Future: Radical Hope in Passion and Pleasure." *Pleasure and Danger*. (1984)

Hunter, Nan D. "Contextualizing the Sexuality Debates: A Chronology." *Sex Wars: Sexual Dissent and Political Culture*. (1995)

Lorde, Audre. "Age, Race, Class and Sex: Women Redefining Difference." *Sister Outsider*. (1984)

Moraga, Cherríe. "La Güera." *Loving in the War Years*. (1983)

Peiss, Kathy. "'Charity Girls' and City Pleasures: Historical Notes on Working-Class Sexuality, 1880-1920." *Powers of Desire: The Politics of Sexuality*. (1983)

Rupp, Leila. J. "'Imagine My Surprise': Women's Relationships in Historical Perspective." *Frontiers: A Journal of Women's Studies*. (1980)

Schneider, Beth E. and Valerie Jenness. "Social Control, Civil Liberties, and Women's Sexuality." *Women Resisting AIDS: Feminist Strategies of Empowerment*. (1995)

Sharonrose, Dánahy. "Myths/Realities of Bisexuality." *Bi Any Other Name: Bisexual People Speak Out*. (1989)

Thompson, Sharon. "Introduction." *Teenage Girls' Tales of Sex, Romance, and Pregnancy*. (1995)

Tilley, Christine M. "Sexuality in Women with Physical Disabilites: A Social Justice or Health Issue?" *Sexuality & Disability* (1996)

Violence

By Willa Young

Allen, Robert L. and Paul Kivel. "Men Changing Men." *Ms*. (1994)

Allison, Dorothy. "Mama." *Trash*. (1988)

Anderson, Margaret. "Recovery From Violence." *Dating Violence: Young Women in Danger*. (1991)

"Anishinabe Values/Social Law Regarding Wife Battering." *Indigenous Woman.* (1992)

Excerpts from Minneapolis Ordinance 83-Or-323 Amending Title 7, Chapter 139 of the Minneapolis Code of Ordinances relating to Civil Rights: In General. (1983)

Bernstein, Nina. "College Campuses Hold Court in the Shadow of Mixed Loyalities." *The New York Times.* (1996)

"Breaking the Cycle: The Violence Against Women Act." *Issues Quarterly.* (1994)

Coronel, Sheila and Ninotchka Rosca. "For the Boys: Filipinas Expose Years of Sexual Slavery by the U.S. and Japan." *Ms.* (1993)

D.G. "Domestic Violence: What's Love Got to Do with It?" *Ms.* (1994)

Duggan, Lisa, Nan D. Hunter and Carole S. Vance. "False Promises: Feminist Antipornography Legislation." *Sex Wars: Sexual Dissent and Political Culture.* (1992)

Duggan, Lisa. "Feminist Historians and Antipornography Campaigns: An Overview." Adapted from a speech given at The Sex Panic: A Conference on Women, Censorship and "Pornography" May 7–8, 1993.

Hill, Steven and Nina Silver. "Civil Rights Antipornography Legislation: Addressing the Harm to Women." *Transforming a Rape Culture.* (1993)

Hurston, Zora Neale. "Sweat."*Fire.* (1926)

Kimmel, Michael S. "Clarence, William, Iron Mike, Tailhook, Senator Packwood, Spur Posse, Magic . . . And Us." *Transforming a Rape Culture.* (1993)

Marcus, Sharon. "Fighting Bodies, Fighting Words: A Theory and Politics of Rape Prevention." *Feminists Theorize the Political.* (1992)

Michals, Debra. "Cyber-Rape: How Virtual Is It?" *Ms.* (1997)

NiCarthy, Ginny. "Addictive Love and Abuse." *Dating Violence, Young Women in Danger.* (1991)

Obejas, Achy. "Women Who Batter Women." *Ms.* (1994)

Pfister, Bonnie. "Swept Awake! Negotiating Passion on Campus." *On the Issues: The Progressive Woman's Quarterly.* (1994)

Roberts, Albert. "Introduction: Myths and Realities Regarding Battered Women." *Helping Battered Women: New Perspectives and Remedies.* (1996)

Warshaw, Robin. "Introduction." *I Never Called it Rape.* (1988)

Warshaw, Robin. "The Reality of Acquaintance Rape" *I Never Called it Rape.* (1988)

Zambrano, Myrna. "Social and Cultural Reasons for Abuse." *Mejor Sula Que Mal Acompanada.* (1985)

Women, Representation and Culture

By Judith Mayne

Bovenschen, Silvia. "Is There a Feminine Aesthetic?" *New German Critique.* (1977)

Brubach, Holly. "The Athletic Esthetic." *The New York Times Magazine.* (1996)

Chadwick, Whitney. "Women Who Run with the Brushes & Glue." *Confessions of the Guerrilla Girls.* (1995)

"Changing Beauty Norms." *Godey's Lady's Book* and *Harper's Bazaar.* (1848/1908)

Chernik, Abra Fortune. "The Body Politic." *Listen Up!: Voices from the Next Feminist Generation.* (1995)

Clifton, Lucille. "Homage to My Hips" (1980) & "Homage to My Hair"(1987)

Davis, Angela. "I Used to Be Your Sweet Mama: Ideology, Sexuality and Domesticity in the Blues of Gertrude 'Ma' Rainey and Bessie Smith." *Sexy Bodies: The Strange Carnalities of Feminism.* (1995)

Douglas, Susan. "Why the Shirelles Mattered." *Where the Girls Are: Growing Up Female with the Mass Media.* (1994)

France, Kim. "Feminism Amplified." *New York Magazine.* (1996)

Frueh, Joanna. "The Body Through Women's Eyes." *The Power of Feminist Art: The American Movement of the 1970s, History and Impact.* (1994).

Mayne, Judith. "Fear of Falling." *Women on Ice.* (1995)

Middlebrook, Diane Wood. "The Artful Voyeur: Anna Deavere Smith and Henry Louis Gates, Jr., on Private Life and Public Art." *Transition.* (1995)

Minkowitz, Donna. "Xena: She's Big, Tall, Strong—and Popular." *Ms.* (1996)

Rapping, Elayne. "Feminist Theory and the TV Movies: What the Genre Does Best." *The Movie of the Week: Private Stories, Public Events.* (1992)

Rowe, Kathleen. "Roseanne: The Unruly Woman as Domestic Goddess." *The Unruly Woman.* (1995)

Schwartz, Therese. "The History of Women's Art: Sins of the Omission and Revisions." *Helicon Nine.* (1986)

Stein, Judith. "Collaboration." *The Power of Feminist Art: The American Movement of the 1970s History and Impact.* (1994)

Walker, Alice. "In Search of Our Mothers' Gardens." In Search of Our Mothers' Gardens. (1983)

Wilson, Leigh and Jeanne Albronda Heaton. "Talk TV: How Women's Issues are Turned into Trash." *Ms.* (1995)

Wolf, Naomi. Excerpt from *The Beauty Myth.* (1991)

Woolf, Virginia. "The Story of Shakespeares's Sister." *A Room of One's Own.* (1929)

Yamamoto, Hisaye. "Seventeen Syllables." *Seventeen Syllables and Other Stories.* (1988)

Work, Poverty and Economic Policy

By Mary Margaret Fonow

"We Are Family." *Issues Quarterly*. (1996)

Bem, Sandra Lipsitz. Excerpt from *The Lenses of Gender*. (1993)

Bernstein, Nina. "Study Says Equality Eludes Most Women in Law Firms." *The New York Times*. (1996)

Bray, Rosemary. "So How Did I Get Here?" *The New York Times*. (1992)

Carvajal, Doreen. "For Immigrant Maids, Not a Job but Servitude." *The New York Times*. (1996)

Cobble, Dorothy Sue. "Peculiarities of Service Work: A Room, Meals, and Tips." *Dishing it Out: Waitresses and Their Unions in the Twentieth Century*. (1991)

Enloe, Cynthia. "The Globetrotting Sneaker." *Ms*. (1995)

"Facts on Working Women." U.S. Dept. Of Labor, Women's Bureau. (1996)

"Good For Business: Making Full Use of the Nation's Human Capital—A Fact-Finding Report of the Federal Glass Ceiling Commission." (1995)

Gooding, Cheryl and Pat Reeve. "The Fruits of Our Labor: Women in the Labor Movement. *Social Policy*. (1993)

Hochschild, Arlie. "Men Who Do and Men Who Don't." *The Second Shift: Working Parents and the Revolution at Home*. (1989)

Hurston, Zora Neale. "Sweat." *Fire*. (1926)

IWPR (Institute for Women's Policy Research). "Few Welfare Moms Fit the Stereotypes." (1995)

IWPR (Institute for Women's Policy Research). "State of the States: Women & Economic Security." (1995)

Kessler-Harris, Alice. "The Meaning of Work in Women's Lives." *Women Have Always Worked: A Historical Overview*. (1981)

Lii, Jane H. "Week in Sweatshop Reveals Grim Conspiracy of the Poor." *The New York Times.* (1995)

Moore, Marat. "Walk in Beauty: Interview with Evelyn Luna (Evie Tsosie)." *Women in the Mines: Stories of Life and Work.* (1996)

Moore, Marat. "Introduction." *Women in the Mines: Stories of Life and Work.* (1996)

National Foundation of Women Business Owners. "Women-Owned Businesses in the United States: 1996—A Fact Sheet."

Redwood, Rene. "Are Women Really Moving Up?" *The Washington Post.* (1995)

"War Work." *America's Working Women: A Documentary History 1600 to the Present.* (1976)

"Working Conditions in Early Factories, 1845." Excerpted from "The First Official Investigation of Labor Conditions in Massachusetts." *A Documentary History of American Industrial Society.* (1910)

Contents

Difference and Inequality

Mary Margaret Fonow

Difference is a basic fact of life. How we deal with difference as individuals and as a society may very well be the distinguishing characteristics of our time. Is difference considered the basis of inequality, the criterion of exclusion, the measuring rod that separates you from others? Or is the acceptance of difference the foundation of a multicultural society, a strength to build upon, the appreciation of which helps us to see what we have in common with others? Is difference something to be embraced or something to be feared?

There are a number of ways to think about difference. Personality differences, individual talent, and a variety of life experiences make us unique, add interest to our relationships and organizations, and can be the envy of others. Other types of difference such as age, sex, race, religion, nationality, and sexual orientation are important ingredients in our rich national culture and help us to define who we are individually and collectively as a people. However, these same differences can also be the basis of stereotyping, prejudice and discrimination, and it is this negative use of difference that alarms feminists. How did these categories of difference become the foundation for inequality and domination? What gives difference meaning? How do the categories of difference relate to each other? How do the multiple categories of difference intersect with each other in the lives of women? How does difference construct advantages as well as disadvantages? How are the norms against which some individuals are measured and classified as different created and maintained?

The United States has always been a racially and culturally diverse society. Its diversity was achieved through the conquest of Native Americans, the annexation of large parts of Mexico, the enslavement of Africans, as well as through immigration from many different regions of the world. Immigrants fleeing war, religious persecution, political oppression, famine, and poverty come to the U.S. to seek a better life and to fuel the economy's need for cheap labor to build railroads, mine copper, produce garments, harvest crops, and perform domestic service. The process of being uprooted and transplanted—forcibly or because of the lack of alternatives—provides America a complicated if rich multicultural history as well as a framework for understanding contemporary feminism.

By the year 2060 no one racial group in the U.S. will be the numerically dominant group. This is already the case in some regions of the country such as Texas, Florida, New Mexico, and California. Latinos are the fastest growing group and this will be the pattern for some time to come. Each younger generation is more racially diverse than the one before it and this trend will continue. For example, 84% of the population between the ages of 50 to 59 are white, while 74% of the population under 9 is white. Immigration is at an all time peak surpassing our greatest period of immigration. The majority of these immigrants come from countries in Asia and Latin America. Increasing numbers of the population are members of more than one racial group. The number of children of interracial families tripled between 1970 and 1990, reaching about 2 million. By the year 2000 the majority of new workers will be men of color and women. Economically the U.S. is also characterized by wide disparities in income creating sharp divisions in our opportunity structure. There are an estimated 43 million people with disabilities. The gay, lesbian and bisexual population, while hard to measure, is estimated to be about 10% of the population in the 12 largest metropolitan areas. It is impossible to understand women's lives and experiences without understanding how gender is shaped by race, class, culture and ethnicity, sexual orientation and disability status.

Throughout history feminist scholars and activists have made intellectual and political claims about women's similarity to and difference from men. The tension between these two poles, sameness and difference, has been a part of the women's movement since the 18th century. Early advocates of women's rights argued that since women had the same capacity to reason as men they were therefore entitled to the same democratic rights as men. In the late 19th century the momentum swung the other way and feminists argued that women were different from men and that women's unique character rooted in motherhood made them morally superior to men. Over-preoccupation with differences between men and women can obscure the differences among women. More recent research shows that the life chances and experiences of women of color, lesbians, older women and women with disabilities in our society are simultaneously shaped by multiple structures of inequality making it difficult if not impossible to separate one from another. For example, the unique form of sexism based on the blending of racial and ethnic stereotypes with gender stereotypes has been labeled "ethnic sexism" by sociologist Esther Ngan-Ling Chow. Stereotypes of Jewish American princesses, Asian picture brides, or sexually seductive Black and Latin women serve to re-enforce power differentials based on both gender and race.

Because sexism and other forms of discrimination operate on many levels including individual, organizational, institutional, and cultural, it is hard to conceptualize how it works. At the individual level discrimination and prejudice involve unequal treatment and stereotyping on a one-to-one basis and are targeted to a specific individual. A teacher who relates to an individual student on the basis of her membership in a particular racial or ethnic category would be engaging in interpersonal discrimination, ie., lowering academic expectations or making assumptions about an individual student's abilities based on skin color. Other types of disadvantage are woven into the practices, rules and policies of organizations or can become so pervasive and widespread as to become institutionalized in the very way society is organized. These discriminatory practices disadvantage entire groups and classes of people. Heterosexism is built into employment practices. For example, lesbian teachers and professors cannot claim health benefits for their domestic partners. Finally, discrimination based on difference can become part and parcel of the cultural fabric of society by pervading our norms, values, language, symbols, and artistic and cultural products. Creating a

3

multicultural curriculum inclusive of the experiences and cultural expressions of women from a range of diverse backgrounds helps us to understand the cultural significance of difference.

Difference can also be the location of creativity, knowledge and energy. Women artists, musicians, and writers have captured the rich cultural fabric of difference. Some use their talents and experiences of difference as a source of insight, pride and even spiritual development. Creative writer, Judith Ortiz Cofer, uses poetry as a way of exploring difference and connecting across differences.

Others find strength and purpose in the struggle against discrimination and domination on the basis of differences. Besides working as a source of creative energy for artists, difference also can be a catalyst for social change. A good example is disability rights. Historically, people with disabilities (psychological and/or physical) have been denied educational, social, economic and cultural opportunities. While civil rights for people with disabilities have become increasingly available, it was not until the passage of the Americans with Disabilities Act in 1990 that certain rights were available for all who have disabilities. Now, whether one is permanently or temporarily disabled, regardless of the nature of the disability, one has a right to receive an education, be treated fairly in the job market, and have access to all public facilities and buildings. Access has improved transportation and public services for more than the nation's disabled. Such accommodations have improved the quality of life for all who use them.

Manning Marable, a political theorist and the Director of the Institute for Research in African-American Studies at Columbia University, reminds us "difference and diversity do not have to be translated into inferiority and subordination. Difference provides an opportunity for learning about others and ourselves. The exploration of difference helps us to understand what value we hold in common." He contends that if we learn to embrace the other in ourselves we can reconcile diversity and difference with the fullest meaning of democracy. We already have a diverse society. There is no need for individuals to define who they are by diminishing the humanity of someone perceived to be different. We can live and thrive with our differences if we are willing to acknowledge the past and work toward the elimination of the inequality based on difference. Difference is not the problem. It is using difference as the basis of organizing the opportunities and rewards in society that is the problem. The poet and essayist, Audre Lorde, a woman who was comfortable with many forms of difference, proclaimed, "My fullest concentration of energy is available to me only when I integrate all the parts of who I am, openly, allowing power from particular sources of my living to flow back and forth freely through all my different selves, without the restrictions of externally imposed definition."

FURTHER READINGS

Anzaldua, Gloria. 1987. *Borderlands/La Frontera: The New Mestiza.* San Francisco: Spinsters/Aunt Lute.

Benokraitis, Nijole V. (Ed.) 1997. *Subtle Sexism: Current Practice and Prospects for Change.* Thousand Oaks, CA: Sage Publications.

Drakulic, Slavenka. 1993. *The Balkan Express: Fragments form the Other Side of War.* New York: W.W. Norton.

Grealy, Lucy. 1995. *Autobiography of a Face.* New York: Harperperennial.

Golden, Marita and Susan Richards Shreve. (Eds.) 1995. *Skin Deep: Black Women & White Women Write About Race.* New York: Doubleday.

hooks, bell. 1996. *Reel to Real: Race, Sex, and Class at the Movies.* New York: Routledge.

Kim, Elaine H., Lilia V. Villanueva, Asian Women United. 1997. *Making More Waves: New Writing by Asian American Women.* Boston: Beacon.

Lazarre, Jane. 1997. *Beyond the Whiteness of Whiteness: Memoir of a White Mother of Black Sons.* Durham: Duke University Press.

Maracle, Lee. 1993. *Ravensong: A Novel.* Vancouver: Press Gang Publishers.

Rothenberg, Paula S. (Ed.) 1997. *Race, class, and gender in the United States.* New York: St. Martin's.

Thompson, Becky and Sangeeta Tyagi. (Eds.) 1996. *Names We Call Home: Autobiography on Racial Identity.* New York: Routledge.

Silko, Leslie Marmon. 1996. *Yellow Woman and a Beauty of the Spirit: Essays on Native American Life Today.* Simon & Schuster: Touchstone.

Zinn, Maxine Baca and Bonnie Thornton Dill. 1994. *Women of Color in U.S. Society.* Philadelphia: Temple University Press.

THE OTHER BODY: REFLECTIONS ON DIFFERENCE, DISABILITY, AND IDENTITY POLITICS (1993)

Ynestra King

As Ynestra King suggests in the following 1993 essay, disability is the only category of "difference" that "can happen to anyone in an instant, transforming that person's life and identity forever." A troubling idea in a culture that views "autonomy" and disability as opposites, King demonstrates through her own experiences with disability how fears and cultural expectations about the human body shape the way women with disabilities are treated.

Disabled people rarely appear in popular culture. When they do, their disability must be a continuous preoccupation overshadowing all other areas of their character. Disabled people are disabled. That is what they "do." That is what they "are."

My own experience with a mobility impairment that is only minorly disfiguring is that one must either be a creature of the disability, or have transcended it entirely. For me, like most disabled people (and this of course depends on relative severity), neither extreme is true. It is an organic, literally embodied fact that will not change—like being a woman. While it may be possible to "do gender," one does not "do disability." But there is an organic base to both conditions that extends far into culture, and the meaning that "nature" has. Unlike being a woman, being disabled is not a socially constructed condition. It is a tragedy of nature, of a kind that will always exist. The very condition of disability provides a vantage point of a certain lived experience in the body, a lifetime of opportunity for the observation of reaction to bodily deviance, a testing ground for reactions to persons who are readily perceived as having something wrong or being different. It is fascinating, maddening, and disorienting. It defies categories of "sickness" and "health," "broken" and "whole." It is in between.

Meeting people has an overlay: I know what they notice first is that I am different. And there is the experience of the difference in another person's reaction who meets me sitting down (when the disability is not apparent), and standing up and walking (when the infirmity is obvious). It is especially noticeable when another individual is flirting and flattering, and has an abrupt change in affect when I stand up. I always make sure that I walk around in front of someone before I accept a date, just to save face for both of us. Once the other person perceives the disability, the switch on the sexual circuit breaker often pops off—the connection is broken. "Chemistry" is over. I have a lifetime of such experiences, and so does every other disabled woman I know.

White middle-class people—especially white men—in the so-called First World have the most negative reactions. And I always recognize studied politeness, the attempt to pretend that there's nothing to notice (this is the liberal response—Oh, You're black? I hadn't noticed). Then there's the do-gooder response, where the person falls all over her/himself, insisting on doing everything for you; later they hate you; it's a form of objectification. It conveys to you that that is all they see, rather like a man who can't quit talking with a woman about sex.

In the era of identity politics in feminism, disability has not only been an added cross to bear, but an added "identity" to take on—with politically correct positions, presumed instant alliances, caucuses to join, and closets to come out of. For example, I was once dragged across a room to meet someone. My friend, a very politically correct lesbian feminist, said, "She's disabled, too. I thought you'd like to meet her." Rather than argue—what would I say? "I'm not interested in other disabled people," or "This is my night off"? (The truth in that moment was like the truth of this experience in every other moment, complicated and difficult to explain.)—I went along to find myself standing before someone strapped in a wheelchair she propels by blowing into a tube with a respirator permanently fastened to the back of the chair. To suggest that our relative experience of disability is something we could casually compare (as other people stand by!) demonstrates the crudity of perception about the complex nature of bodily experience.

My infirmity is partial leg paralysis. I can walk anywhere, climb stairs, drive a car, ride a horse, swim, hang-glide, fly a plane, hike in the wilderness, go to jail for my political convictions, travel alone, and operate heavy equipment. I can earn a living, shop, cook, eat as I please, dress myself, wash and iron my own clothes, clean my house. The woman in that wheelchair can do none of these fundamental things, much less the more exotic ones. On a more basic human level I can spontaneously get my clothes off if I decide to make love. Once in bed my lover and I can forget my disability. None of this is true of the woman in the wheelchair. There is no bodily human activity that does not have to be specially negotiated, none in which she is not absolutely "different." It would take a very long time, and a highly nuanced conversation, for us to be able to share experiences as if they were common. The experience of disability for the two of us was more different than my experience is from the daily experience of people who are not considered disabled. So much for disability solidarity.

With disability, one is somewhere on a continuum between total bodily dysfunction—or death—and complete physical wholeness. In some way, this probably applies to every living person. So when is it that we call a person "disabled"? When do they become "other"? There are "minor" disabilities that are nonetheless significant for a person's life. Color blindness is one example. But in our culture, color blindness is considered an inconvenience rather than a disability.

The ostracization, marginalization, and distorted response to disability are not simply issues of prejudice and denial of civil rights. They reflect attitudes toward bodily life, an unease in the human skin, an inability to cope with contingency, ambiguity, flux, finitude, and death.

Visibly disabled people (like women) in this culture are the scapegoats for resentments of the limitations of organic life. I had polio when I was seven, finishing second grade. I had excelled in everything, and rarely missed school. I had one bad conduct notation—for stomping on the boys' blocks when they wouldn't let me play with them. Although I had leg braces and crutches when I was ready to start school next year, I wanted desperately to go back and resume as much of the same life as I could. What I was not prepared for was the response of the school system. They insisted that I was now "handicapped" and should go into what they called "special education." This was a program aimed primarily at multiply disabled children, virtually all of whom were mentally retarded as well as physically disabled. It was in a separate wing of another school, and the children were completely segregated from the "normal" children in every aspect of the school day, including lunch and recreational activities. I was fortunate enough to have educated, articulate parents and an especially aggressive mother; she went to the school board and waged a tireless campaign to allow me to come back to my old school on a trial basis—the understanding being that the school could send me to special education if things "didn't work out" in the regular classroom.

And so began my career as an "exceptional" disabled person, not like the *other* "others." And I was glad. I didn't want to be associated with those others either. Apart from the objective limitations caused by the polio, the transformation in identity—the difference in worldly reception—was terrifying and embarrassing, and it went far beyond the necessary considerations my limitations required.

My experience as "other" is much greater and more painful as a disabled person than as a woman. Maybe the most telling dimension of this knowledge is my observation of the reactions of others over the years, of how deeply afraid people are of being outside the normative appearance (which is getting narrower as capitalism exaggerates patriarchy). It is no longer enough to be thin; one must have ubiquitous muscle definition, nothing loose, flabby, or ill defined, no fuzzy boundaries. And of course, there's the importance of control. Control over aging, bodily process, weight, fertility, muscle tone, skin quality, and movement. Disabled women, regardless of how thin, are without full bodily control.

I see disabled women fight these normative standards in different ways, but never get free of negotiating and renegotiating them. I did it by constructing my life around other values and, to the extent possible, developing erotic attachments to people who had similar values, and for whom my compensations were more than adequate. But at one point, after two disastrous but steamy liaisons with a champion athlete and a dancer (during which my friends pointed out the obvious unkind truth and predicted painful endings), I discovered the worlds I have tried to protect myself from: the disastrous attraction to "others" to complete oneself. I have seen disabled women endure unspeakably horrible relationships because they were so flattered to have such a conventionally attractive individual in tow.

And then there's the weight issue. I got fat by refusing to pay attention to my body. Now that I'm slimming down again, my old vanities and insecurities are surfacing. The battle of dieting can be especially fraught for disabled women. It is more difficult because exercising is more difficult, as is traveling around to get the proper foods, and then preparing them. But the underlying rage at the system that makes you feel as if you *are* your body (female, infirm) and that everything else is window dressing—this also undermines the requisite discipline. A tempting response is to resort to an ideal of self as bodiless essence in which the body is completely incidental, and irrelevant.

The wish that the body should be irrelevant has been one of my most fervent lifelong wishes. The knowledge that it isn't is my most intense lifelong experience.

I have seen other disabled women wear intentionally provocative clothes, like the woman in the wheelchair on my bus route to work. She can barely move. She has a pretty face, and tiny legs she could not possibly walk on. Yet she wears black lace stockings and spike high heels. The other bus occupants smile condescendingly, or pretend not to notice, or whisper in appalled disbelief that this woman could represent herself as having a sexual self. That she could "flaunt" her sexual being violates the code of acceptable appearance for a disabled woman. This woman's apparel is no more far out than that of many other women on our bus—but she refuses to fold up and be a good little asexual handicapped person.

The well-intentioned liberal new campaigns around "hire the handicapped" are oppressive in related ways. The Other does not only have to demonstrate her competence on insider terms; she must be better, by way of apologizing for being different and rewarding the insiders for letting her in. And the happy handicapped person, who has had faith placed in her/him, must vindicate "the race" because the politics of tokenism assumes that there are in fact other qualifications than doing the job.

This is especially prejudicial in a recession, where there are few social services, where it is "every man for himself." Disabled people inevitably have greater expenses, since assistance must often be paid for privately. In the U.S., public construction of the disabled body is that one either is fully disabled and dysfunctional/unemployable (and therefore eligible for public welfare) or totally on one's own. There is no in-between—the possibility of a little assistance, or exceptions in certain areas. Disabled people on public assistance cannot work or they will lose their benefits. (In the U.S. ideology that shapes public attitudes and public policy, one is either fully dependent or fully autonomous.) But the reality of human organic life is that everyone is different in some way; there is no such thing as a totally autonomous individual. Yet the mythology of autonomy perpetuates in terrible ways the oppression of the disabled. It also perpetuates misogyny—and the destruction of the planet.

It may be that this clear lack of autonomy—this reminder of mortal finitude and contingency and embeddedness of nature and the body—is at the root of the hatred of the disabled. On the continuum of autonomy and dependence, disabled people need help. To need help is to feel humiliated, to have failed. I think this "help" issue must be even harder for men than women. But any disabled person is always negotiating both the provisionality of autonomy and the rigidity of physical norms.

From the vantage point of disability, there are some objective and desirable aspects of autonomy. But they have to do with independence. The preferred protocol is that the attendant or friend perform the task that the disabled person needs done in the way the disabled person *asks it to be done.* Assistance from friends and family is a negotiated process, and often maddening. For that reason most disabled people prefer to live in situations where they can do all the basic functions themselves, with whatever special equipment or built-ins are required.

It's a dreadful business, this needing help. And it's more dreadful in the U.S. than in any place in the world, because our heroes are dynamic overcomers of adversity, and there is an inevitable cultural contempt for weakness.

Autonomy is on a continuum toward dependency and death. And the idea that dependency could come at any time, that one could die at any time, or be dismembered or disfigured, and still have to live (maybe even *want to live*) is unbearable in a context that understands and values autonomy in the way we moderns do.

I don't want to depict this experience of unbearability as strictly cultural. The compromising of the human body before its natural time is tragic. It forces terrible hardship on the individual to whom it occurs. But the added overlay of oppression on the disabled is intimately related to the fear of death, and the acknowledgment of our embeddedness in organic nature. We are finite, contingent, dependent creatures by our very nature; we will all eventually die. We will all experience compromises to our physical integrity. The aspiration to human wholeness is an oppressive idealism. Socially, it is deeply infantilizing.

It promotes a simplistic view of the human person, a static notion of human life that prevents the maturity and social wisdom that might allow human beings to more fully apprehend the human condition. It marginalizes the "different," those perceived as hopelessly wedded to organic existence—women and the disabled. The New Age "human potential movement"—in the name of maximizing human growth—is one of the worst offenders in obscuring the kind of human growth I am suggesting.

I too believe that the potential for human growth and creativity is infinite—but it is not groundless. The common ground for the person—the human body—is a place of shifting sand that can fail us at any time. It can change shape and properties without warning; this is an essential truth of embodied existence.

Of all the ways of becoming "other" in our society, disability is the only one that can happen to anyone, in an instant, transforming that person's life and identity forever.

QUESTIONS

1. What is King's disability? How is King not like the other "others"? How does she feel about her experiences with disability? How does she feel about identity politics?

2. In what ways is the experience of being a woman similar to being disabled? In what ways are these experiences different? What are some of the unique issues women *with* disabilities face?

3. According to King, disability is more than a civil rights issue. What does she mean by this? Where does she root cultural anxieties about disability? What role does control play?

THE MYTH OF THE LATIN WOMAN: I JUST MET A GIRL NAMED MARÍA (1993)

Judith Ortiz Cofer

In the following narrative from her 1993 book The Latin Deli, *poet Judith Ortiz Cofer describes her various encounters with cultural stereotypes about Latin women. As a Puerto Rican girl growing up in New Jersey, and later as an accomplished adult, Cofer experienced an array of responses to her "difference" and it strengthened her desire to convey a more accurate and more complex portrait of a Latina woman's identity through her writing.*

On a bus trip to London from Oxford University where I was earning some graduate credits one summer, a young man, obviously fresh from a pub, spotted me and as if struck by inspiration went down on his knees in the aisle. With both hands over his heart he broke into an Irish tenor's rendition of "María" from *West Side Story*. My politely amused fellow passengers gave his lovely voice the round of gentle applause it deserved. Though I was not

"The Myth of the Latin Woman: I Just Met a Girl Named Maria," by Judith Ortiz Cofer, reprinted from *The Latin Deli*, 1993, by permission of The University of Georgia Press.

quite as amused, I managed my version of an English smile: no show of teeth, no extreme contortions of the facial muscles—I was at this time of my life practicing reserve and cool. Oh, that British control, how I coveted it. But María had followed me to London, reminding me of a prime fact of my life: you can leave the Island, master the English language, and travel as far as you can, but if you are a Latina, especially one like me who so obviously belongs to Rita Moreno's gene pool, the Island travels with you.

This is sometimes a very good thing—it may win you that extra minute of someone's attention. But with some people, the same things can make *you* an island—not so much a tropical paradise as an Alcatraz, a place nobody wants to visit. As a Puerto Rican girl growing up in the United States and wanting like most children to "belong," I resented the stereotype that my Hispanic appearance called forth from many people I met.

Our family lived in a large urban center in New Jersey during the sixties, where life was designed as a microcosm of my parents' casas on the island. We spoke in Spanish, we ate Puerto Rican food bought at the bodega, and we practiced strict Catholicism complete with Saturday confession and Sunday mass at a church where our parents were accommodated into a one-hour Spanish mass slot, performed by a Chinese priest trained as a missionary for Latin America.

As a girl I was kept under strict surveillance, since virtue and modesty were, by cultural equation, the same as family honor. As a teenager I was instructed on how to behave as a proper señorita. But it was a conflicting message girls got, since the Puerto Rican mothers also encouraged their daughters to look and act like women and to dress in clothes our Anglo friends and their mothers found too "mature" for our age. It was, and is, cultural, yet I often felt humiliated when I appeared at an American friend's party wearing a dress more suitable to a semiformal than to a playroom birthday celebration. At Puerto Rican festivities, neither the music nor the colors we wore could be too loud. I still experience a vague sense of letdown when I'm invited to a "party" and it turns out to be a marathon conversation in hushed tones rather than a fiesta with salsa, laughter, and dancing—the kind of celebration I remember from my childhood.

I remember Career Day in our high school, when teachers told us to come dressed as if for a job interview. It quickly became obvious that to the barrio girls, "dressing up" sometimes meant wearing ornate jewelry and clothing that would be more appropriate (by mainstream standards) for the company Christmas party than as daily office attire. That morning I had agonized in front of my closet, trying to figure out what a "career girl" would wear because, essentially, except for Marlo Thomas on TV, I had no models on which to base my decision. I knew how to dress for school: at the Catholic school I attended we all wore uniforms; I knew how to dress for Sunday mass, and I knew what dresses to wear for parties at my relatives' homes. Though I do not recall the precise details of my Career Day outfit, it must have been a composite of the above choices. But I remember a comment my friend (an Italian-American) made in later years that coalesced my impressions of that day. She said that at the business school she was attending the Puerto Rican girls always stood out for wearing "everything at once." She meant, of course, too much jewelry, too many accessories. On that day at school, we were simply made the negative models by the nuns who were themselves not credible fashion experts to any of us. But it was painfully obvious to me that to the others, in their tailored skirts and silk blouses, we must have seemed "hopeless" and "vulgar." Though I now know that most adolescents feel out of step much of the time, I also know that for the Puerto Rican girls of my generation that sense was intensified. The way our teachers and classmates looked at us that day in school was just a taste of the culture clash that awaited us in the real world, where prospective employers and men on the street would often misinterpret our tight skirts and jingling bracelets as a come-on.

Mixed cultural signals have perpetuated certain stereotypes—for example, that of the Hispanic woman as the "Hot Tamale" or sexual firebrand. It is a one-dimensional view that the media have found easy to promote. In their special vocabulary, advertisers have designated "sizzling" and "smoldering" as the adjectives of choice for describing not only the foods but also the women of Latin America. From conversations in my house I recall hearing about the harassment that Puerto Rican women endured in factories where the "boss men" talked to them as if sexual innuendo was all they understood and, worse, often gave them the choice of submitting to advances or being fired.

It is custom, however, not chromosomes, that leads us to choose scarlet over pale pink. As young girls, we were influenced in our decisions about clothes and colors by the women—older sisters and mothers who had grown up on a tropical island where the natural environment was a riot of primary colors, where showing your skin was one way to keep cool as well as to look sexy. Most important of all, on the island, women perhaps felt freer to dress and move more provocatively, since, in most cases, they were protected by the traditions, mores, and laws of a Spanish/Catholic system of morality and machismo whose main rule was: *You may look at my sister, but if you touch her I will kill you.* The extended family and church structure could provide a young woman with a circle of safety in her small pueblo on the island; if a man "wronged" a girl, everyone would close in to save her family honor.

This is what I have gleaned from my discussions as an adult with older Puerto Rican women. They have told me about dressing in their best party clothes on Saturday nights and going to the town's plaza to promenade with their girlfriends in front of the boys they liked. The males were thus given an opportunity to admire the women and to express their admiration in the form of *piropos:* erotically charged street poems they composed on the spot. I have been subjected to a few piropos while visiting the Island, and they can be outrageous, although custom dictates that they must never cross into obscenity. This ritual, as I understand it, also entails a show of studied indifference on the woman's part; if she is "decent," she must not acknowledge the man's impassioned words. So I do understand how things can be lost in translation. When a Puerto Rican girl dressed in her idea of what is attractive meets a man from the mainstream culture who has been trained to react to certain types of clothing as a sexual signal, a clash is likely to take place. The line I first heard based on this aspect of the myth happened when the boy who took me to my first formal dance leaned over to plant a sloppy overeager kiss painfully on my mouth, and when I didn't respond with sufficient passion said in a resentful tone: "I thought you Latin girls were supposed to mature early"—my first instance of being thought of as a fruit or vegetable—I was supposed to *ripen* not just grow into womanhood like other girls.

It is surprising to some of my professional friends that some people, including those who should know better, still put others "in their place." Though rarer, these incidents are still commonplace in my life. It happened to me most recently during a stay at a very classy metropolitan hotel favored by young professional couples for their weddings. Late one evening after the theater, as I walked toward my room with my new colleague (a woman with whom I was coordinating an arts program), a middle-aged man in a tuxedo, a young girl in satin and lace on his arm, stepped directly into our path. With his champagne glass extended toward me, he exclaimed, "Evita!"

Our way blocked, my companion and I listened as the man half-recited, half-bellowed "Don't Cry for Me, Argentina." When he finished, the young girl said: "How about a round of applause for my daddy?" We complied, hoping this would bring the silly spectacle to a close. I was becoming aware that our little group was attracting the attention of the other guests. "Daddy" must have perceived this too, and he once more barred the way as we tried to walk past him. He began to shout-sing a ditty to the tune of "La Bamba"—except the lyrics were about a girl named María whose exploits all rhymed with her name and gonorrhea. The girl kept saying "Oh, Daddy" and looking at me with pleading eyes. She wanted me to laugh along with the others. My companion and I stood silently waiting for the man to end his offensive song. When he finished, I looked not at him but at his daughter. I advised her calmly never to ask her father what he had done in the army. Then I walked between them and to my room. My friend complimented me on my cool handling of the situation. I confessed to her that I really had wanted to push the jerk into the swimming pool. I knew that this same man—probably a corporate executive, well educated, even worldly by most standards—would not have been likely to regale a white woman with a dirty song in public. He would perhaps have checked his impulse by assuming that she could be somebody's wife or mother, or at least *somebody* who might take offense. But to him, I was just an Evita or a María: merely a character in his cartoon-populated universe.

Because of my education and my proficiency with the English language, I have acquired many mechanisms for dealing with the anger I experience. This was not true for my parents, nor is it true for the many Latin women working at menial jobs who must put up with stereotypes about our ethnic group such as: "They make good domestics." This is another facet of the myth of the Latin woman in the United States. Its origin is simple to deduce. Work as domestics, waitressing, and factory jobs are all that's available to women with little English and few skills. The myth of the Hispanic menial has been sustained by the same media phenomenon that made "Mammy" from *Gone with the Wind* America's idea of the black woman for generations; María, the housemaid or counter girl, is now indelibly etched into the national psyche. The big and the little screens have presented us with the picture of the funny Hispanic maid, mispronouncing words and cooking up a spicy storm in a shiny California kitchen.

This media-engendered image of the Latina in the United States has been documented by feminist Hispanic scholars, who claim that such portrayals are partially responsible for the denial of opportunities for upward mobility among Latinas in the professions. I have a Chicana friend working on a Ph.D. in philosophy at a major university. She says her doctor still shakes his head in puzzled amazement at all the "big words" she uses. Since I do not wear my diplomas around my neck for all to see, I too have on occasion been sent to that "kitchen," where some think I obviously belong.

One such incident that has stayed with me, though I recognize it as a minor offense, happened on the day of my first public poetry reading. It took place in Miami in a boat-restaurant where we were having lunch before the event. I was nervous and excited as I walked in with my notebook in my hand. An older woman motioned me to her table. Thinking (foolish me) that she wanted me to autograph a copy of my brand new slender volume of verse, I went over. She ordered a cup of coffee from me, assuming that I was the waitress. Easy enough to mistake my poems for menus, I suppose. I know that it wasn't an intentional act of cruelty, yet of all the good things that happened that day, I remember that scene most clearly, because it reminded me of what I had to overcome before anyone would take me seriously. In retrospect I understand that my anger gave my reading fire, that I have almost always taken doubts in my abilities as a challenge—and that the result is, most times, a feeling of satisfaction at having won a convert when I see the cold, appraising eyes warm to my words, the body language change, the smile that indicates that I have opened some avenue for communication. That day I read to that woman and her lowered eyes told me that she was embarrassed at her little faux pas, and when I willed her to look up at me, it was my victory, and she graciously allowed me to punish her with my full attention. We shook hands at the end of the reading, and I never saw her again. She has probably forgotten the whole thing, but maybe not.

Yet I am one of the lucky ones. My parents made it possible for me to acquire a stronger footing in the mainstream culture by giving me the chance at an education. And books and art have saved me from the harsher forms of ethnic and racial prejudice that many of my Hispanic *compañeras* have had to endure. I travel a lot around the United States, reading from my books of poetry and my novel, and the reception I most often receive is one of positive interest by people who want to know more about my culture. There are, however, thousands of Latinas without the privilege of an education or the entrée into society that I have. For them life is a struggle against the misconceptions perpetuated by the myth of the Latina as whore, domestic, or criminal. We cannot change this by legislating the way people look at us. The transformation, as I see it, has to occur at a much more individual level. My personal goal in my public life is to try to replace the old pervasive stereotypes and myths about Latinas with a much more interesting set of realities. Every time I give a reading, I hope the stories I tell, the dreams and fears I examine in my work, can achieve some universal truth which will get my audience past the particulars of my skin color, my accent, or my clothes.

I once wrote a poem in which I called us Latinas "God's brown daughters." This poem is really a prayer of sorts, offered upward, but also, through the human-to-human channel of art, outward. It is a prayer for communication, and for respect. In it, Latin women pray "in Spanish to an Anglo God/with a Jewish heritage," and they are "fervently hoping/that if not omnipotent,/at least He be bilingual."

QUESTIONS

1. How does Cofer describe herself? How is she "different"? How does she feel about her identity? How are her experiences similar to other Latin women she mentions? How are they different? (Or, how is her difference "different"?) What emotions are conveyed in Cofer's narrative?

2. What are some of the specific ethnic stereotypes about Latin women that Cofer encounters? How does she manage these interactions? What is accomplished? Why does Cofer find the stereotyping of Latin women problematic?

3. How do stereotypes function in our society? How do mixed cultural signals compound the problem?

AFFIRMING DIVERSITY: BUILDING A NATIONAL COMMUNITY THAT WORKS (1996)

Lorraine Kenny

Equal opportunity policies are clustered under the umbrella term "affirmative action." Among the most complicated and emotional debates in our diverse society, affirmative action is little understood. Although affirmative action policies have benefited women of all races, they have not done away with the "glass ceiling" that locks women out of high-paying jobs, or the "sticky floor," which traps them in low-paying service sector jobs. In the following article, Lorraine Kenny, an anthropologist, introduces what the fight over affirmative action is really about. Kenny is the author of Daughters of Suburbia: Growing Up White, Middle-Class and Female *and a guest faculty member of Sarah Lawrence College.*

"Affirming Diversity: Building a National Community That Works," by Lorraine Kenny, reprinted by permission from *Issues Quarterly*, Vol. 1, No. 4, 1996. *Issues Quarterly* is the quarterly journal of The National Council for Research on Women (530 Broadway, 10th Fl, New York, NY 10012).

Above all the political and legal wrangling over affirmative action, an important set of national principles and commitments holds steady. The Constitution provides "equal protection under the law" to *all* U.S. citizens, while history defines the nation as the "land of opportunity" and a place where hard work pays off. Affirmative-action programs and policies turn these and other laws and ideals into real-life practices in the nation's classrooms, workrooms, and executive offices.

So why has affirmative action come under fire in recent months? Why are some calling for its demise, claiming it encourages—even legislates—reverse discrimination, while others, including President Clinton, want to amend it, not end it?

"It is one thing to believe in a meritocracy, and it is another to believe it is here right now," says Reginald Wilson, senior scholar at the American Council on Education and author of "Affirmative Action: Yesterday, Today, and Beyond."[1] "Educating and presenting the facts about affirmative action to the American public is only part of the job ahead. Making sure people realize that many of the things we aspire toward are just that, aspirations, is the other side of the battle," adds Wilson.

Numerous studies support this conclusion: affirmative action is not a done deal. Just as the issue began to heat up in the media, inside the Beltway, and on the Supreme Court, the Federal Glass Ceiling Commission released its fact-finding report, *Good for Business; Making full use of the nation's human capital; The environmental scan.*[2] Based on a series of public hearings, commissioned research reports, surveys with chief executive officers, discussions with focus groups, and analyses of U.S. Bureau of the Census data and other materials, the report demonstrates that there are glass ceilings all over corporate America.

Good for Business presents staggering figures:

> 97 percent of the senior managers of Fortune 1000 industrial and Fortune 500 service companies are white; 95 to 97 percent are male.

> In Fortune 2000 industrial and service companies, only 5 percent of senior managers are women—and of that 5 per-cent, virtually all are white.

> In 1994, only two women were CEOs of Fortune 1000 companies. In 1990, a woman with an MBA from one of the

top 20 business schools earned an average of 12 percent less in her first year of work than her male classmates.

African American men with professional degrees earn only 79 percent and African American women with professional degrees earn only 60 percent of what white men in similar positions earn.[3]

How people are perceived affects how far they advance up the corporate ladder, concludes *Good for Business*. In many instances, stereotypes about women and different ethnic and racial groups still determine who gets hired and who gets promoted. As one corporate executive told Glass Ceiling Commission researchers, "What's important is comfort, chemistry, relationships, and collaborations. That's what makes a shop work. When we find minorities and women who think like we do, we snatch them up."[4] From a business perspective this approach makes sense; from an affirmative-action point of view—one committed to opening up rather than limiting opportunity—it doesn't.

"Thinking like we do" implies that people have the same educational opportunities and that they come to the personnel office with a similar set of values and professional and personal needs. According to the Hudson Institute's landmark report, *Workforce 2000*, between 1987 and the year 2000, "non-whites, women, and immigrants will make up more than five-sixths of the net additions to the workforce," with black women constituting the majority of non-whites.[5] Heeding these projections, many businesses have hired "diversity management" consultants to make cultural differences work for rather than against the bottom line.[6] "The issue of diversity is critical to American businesses," says Michelle Carpenter, director of Work/Family Strategies at Aetna. "We have a competitive advantage over the rest of the world because we have a diverse workforce. . . . We can't afford infighting and segregation," cautions Carpenter.

Misperceptions Do Not a Dialogue Make

Unfortunately, in the midst of the current acrimony, infighting and segregation prevail because the public does not fully comprehend the legal parameters of affirmative action. When governor of

California Pete Wilson issued an executive order on July 1, 1995, to "End Preferential Treatment and Promote Individual Opportunity Based on Merit," he stirred up the already turbulent public discussion on affirmative action by adding misperceptions on top of layers of misunderstandings.

Put simply: affirmative action is not about quotas or hiring, promoting, or admitting unqualified employees or students. It is about actively ensuring that everyone has equal access to quality schools and viable employment and business opportunities and about taking reasonable measures to redress enduring histories of discrimination. Concretely, affirmative action is a set of public policies, laws, and executive orders, as well as voluntary and court-ordered practices designed to promote fairness and diversity. (See *IQ*, Points of Law.)

For the most part, they have. According to the Equal Employment Opportunity Commission—the federal body charged with enforcing civil-rights acts as they pertain to employment—of the more than 10,000 reverse-discrimination cases filed between 1987 and 1994, only 10 percent had merit.[7] Likewise, while affirmative-action policies have opened some doors, at least partially, they do not guarantee future access. When Catalyst, a New York City-based research and advocacy group for business and professional women, tracked the presence of women on corporate boards, they found a mixed bag. The good news: in 1995, 81 percent of Fortune 500 companies had at least one female director, compared with 69 percent in 1993. The bad news: women currently hold only 600 of the 6,274 Fortune 500 board seats available.[8] The world has changed, but not enough to warrant a laissez faire attitude toward making American ideals everyday realities.

Historically, the courts and federal government have only cautiously expanded affirmative-action policies and often sought to keep them in check. Women were not included in President Nixon's 1969 executive order imposing hiring "goals and timetables" on federal building contractors until 1971. In the Bakke decision of 1978, the Supreme Court established that colleges and universities could consider race when admitting students, but they could not use racial quotas. And the Supreme Court's *Adarand Construction v. Pena* ruling on June 12, 1995, did not so much strike down as clarify the limits of affirmative action. The 5–4 vote held that any race-based affirmative-action programs are "constitutional only if they are narrowly tailored measures that further compelling governmental interests."[9] Helen Norton, director of the Equal Opportunity Program at the Women's Legal Defense Fund in Washington, D.C., explains: "Adarand was a setback but not a disaster. The Court made it harder for the federal government to set up affirmative-action programs, but they also made it clear that affirmative action is legal." The spate of headlines and articles pronouncing the end of affirmative action that followed this decision further polarized the mounting public discord.

Hyperbole does not lead to workable solutions. A recent survey sponsored by the Feminist Majority Foundation demonstrates that when people understand that affirmative-action programs seek to level the educational and economic playing fields for women and minorities without resorting to numerical quotas, they overwhelmingly register their support.[10] "People know that discrimination is alive and well," says Fran Buchanan, deputy executive director at Equal Rights Advocates, a group that recently conducted focus groups on affirmative action in California. "When we asked, 'Have you seen discrimination?' people were real clear that they had." As a result, Buchanan advocates making sure the public knows that affirmative action benefits everyone. "It brings hiring practices under scrutiny. . . . *Qualified* used to mean knowing somebody; [under affirmative action] everybody has to have the opportunity to apply, even white men," stresses Buchanan.

Beyond the Rhetoric and Toward Commitments

Affirmative action is a tool not a goal. As with any tool, it can be misused, it needs periodic sharpening, and it doesn't work on its own. Rather than perceiving current anti-affirmative-action efforts as tolling the death of a 30-year civil-rights era, we need to attend to what can be done to turn the principles of affirmative action into policy and common practice. Helen Neuborne, program officer at the Ford Foundation, cautions: "The level playing field language is used without understanding what it is and how it happens. The approach to affirmative action needs to be broad." In other words, equal access is a deceptively simple concept. Though affirmative-action laws have been limited to race and gender (see *IQ*, Points of Law: 1961, Executive Order 10925; 1965, Executive Order 11246; and 1967, Executive Order 11375), anti-discrimination measures have cast wider nets, protecting people on the basis of race, religion, sex, national origin, age, and disability (see *IQ*, Points of Law: 1964 and 1991 civil-rights acts; 1967, Age Discrimination in Employment Act; and 1973, Rehabilitation Act). Opening doors means transforming the nation's institutions to account for people's many differences.

The Primacy of Education

The debate over who gets admitted to state universities and colleges largely focuses on the symptom rather than the problem. Given that currently African Americans and Hispanics constitute 37 percent of California's high school graduates, the fact that the University of California, Berkeley counts only 5.5 percent or 1,127 African Americans and 13.8 percent or 2,800 Hispanics among its more than 21,000 undergraduates raises questions about who gets admitted and why.[11] Do California high schools prepare all their students equally? Furthermore, what happens to these students once they matriculate? How many stay in school? How many find mentors to help them navigate the university and reach their full potential as students and citizens? Recent figures show that six-year graduation rates at Berkeley vary from 59 percent for African Americans, 64 percent for Hispanics, 84 percent for whites, and 88 percent for Asians.[12] To what extent do institutional conditions explain these numbers?

Admissions, retention, and graduation problems are not California's alone. Nationally, 70 percent of African American college students drop out of school, as compared with 40 percent of their classmates from other racial and ethnic backgrounds. Similarly, African Americans rarely exceed 7 percent of the undergraduate student population at elite universities across the country.[13] Reassessments of public education occasioned by the 40th anniversary of the Supreme Court's landmark desegregation case, *Brown v. Board of Education*, found that nationwide nearly 70 percent of all black students attend elementary and secondary schools with mostly black and Hispanic enrollments.[14] Adding these facts together suggests that separate is not equal and not every kid gets a running start.

Despite existing desegregation programs and attempts by some states to distribute state educational dollars evenly across districts, not all public primary and secondary schools are created equal. More needs to be done to ensure that kids of *all* backgrounds—from suburban, rural, and urban school districts alike—acquire comparable academic skills and develop the capacity to do college-level work so that they can imagine and pursue productive and challenging futures for themselves. Only then will we begin to experience the social and economic benefits of a level playing field.

Below Every Glass Ceiling Lies a Sticky Floor

When matters turn to work, dismantling the glass ceiling addresses only half the problem. The "sticky floor" of low-paying, low-mobility jobs curtails the advancement of many more white women and women and men of color than does the CEO old boys network.[15] According to Karen Nussbaum, director of the Women's Bureau, U.S. Department of Labor, "You still find a very large group of women in clerical and low-wage service work, and 75 percent of working women still earn less than $25,000" a year.[16] Of these working women, two-thirds are the principal breadwinners in their families. One-third of the female-headed households live in poverty.[17] And women make up 60 percent of the country's minimum-wage workers. At $4.25 an hour, this wage puts less on the dinner table today than it did 40 years ago.[18] In light of these figures, increasing the minimum wage, making health care and other benefits affordable and accessible, and expanding job-training programs for women and girls of all backgrounds will go a long way toward broadening the reach and effectiveness of affirmative-action and equal-opportunity policies. A tool is only as good as the people who use it. If white women and women of color are not given the skills and resources they need to take advantage of opening doors, equal access is a hollow concept.

Missing Numbers and Double Exclusions

What remains largely unsaid in the haggling over affirmative action is the tenacity with which U.S. institutions discriminate on the basis of race and gender. To a great extent, Congress, the courts, the media, and researchers have placed women of color outside the frame of this critical national discussion. Most talk about "women" and "minorities" without specifying where women of color fall in these breakdowns. If they are counted among "minorities," such numbers only tell half their story. "You're either a woman or a person of color; women of color fall in some nether world, making it difficult to discern if discrimination has happened on the basis of race or gender [or both]. If an employer doesn't need to consider race or gender, women of color experience a double exclusion," notes Fran Buchanan of Equal Rights Advocates.

Existing numbers do tell us that women of color generally fare less well than either white women or men of color. For example, in 1994, for every dollar earned by white men, African American men earned 75 cents, white women earned 72 cents, Hispanic men earned 64 cents, African American women earned 63 cents, and Hispanic women earned only 56 cents.[19] Given this playing field, if the states, federal government, and the Supreme Court hamstring or abolish affirmative-action initiatives, women of color have the most to lose.

The Work-Family Connection

In reassessing affirmative action, the country is indirectly looking at who it is and who it wants to be. If women of color are not an integral part of this analysis, policies will fall short of meeting the demands of the nation's schools, workplace, *and* families. One study, *Defining Work and Family Issues: Listening to the Voices of Women of Color*, by Jennifer Tucker and Leslie R. Wolfe of the Center for Women Policy Studies in Washington, D.C., finds that women of color identify racism and sexism in the workplace as "work and family conflicts."[20] Tucker explains, "Women of color experience work and family and workplace diversity issues as intrinsically linked." While many large companies make work-family consulting services available to their employees, most of these programs attend to the ways family life can interfere with workplace productivity. *Defining Work and Family Issues* shows that when women face sexual harassment and racial discrimination on the job their home lives suffer and in the end so do their employers. Productivity and attendance drop. Women become distracted, angry, unmotivated, and eventually leave their jobs. Tucker recommends that companies encourage collaboration between their work-family and workplace-diversity programs.

Elizabeth Kuhn, regional director at Work/Family Directions, a Boston-based company providing work-family services to hundreds of thousands of employees throughout the country, sees her work as affirmative action. In the early 1980s, Work/Family Directions helped employers meet the childcare needs of their workers. Today they offer advice, training, and resource referrals on topics ranging from caring for elderly parents to parenting adolescents to adopting young children. Through an 800 number, Work/Family Directions responds to about 300,000 calls a year. Kuhn reports that women make 90 percent of the calls pertaining to childcare, 75 percent of those asking about elder care, and 50 percent of those requesting information about college planning. "The primary care for family matters rests with women. There are many reasons that women have not cracked the glass ceiling. A complex strategy is needed to help women advance," observes Kuhn.

Reaching for a Diverse and Equal Future

Part of that strategy entails blocking attempts to annul affirmative-action policies on the federal and state levels. The situation calls for "defensive lobbying," asserts the Women's Legal Defense Fund's (WLDF) Helen Norton. In the past year, WLDF and several other groups have been actively educating members of Congress so that they understand the impact affirmative action has had on educating and employing the nation's women. According to Norton, affirmative action is a "smoke screen," a "diversionary tactic. . . . White men, white women, people of all colors are not doing as well as their parents and they're worried about their kids. [WLDF is] trying to make it clear that this fight shouldn't be about affirmative action but about economic security for everybody. It is much easier to oppose affirmative action than it is to address economic issues," concludes Norton.

By working in coalitions that bridge the women's and civil-rights communities, as well as legal, educational, business, and labor constituencies, women's and civil-rights organizations across the country are attempting to reshape the affirmative-action debate so that the discussion broadens and the solutions multiply.

Affirmative action is about race, gender, and class in America. As such it is everyone's issue and in everyone's best interest. In its first 30 years, it has laid the groundwork for changing the way America does business and educates its population. Using the current public discussion to rearticulate our commitment to affirmative action is the first step toward ensuring that the next 30 years will witness the elimination of the glass ceiling and the sticky floor and the institution of a more equitable public-education system and more effective work-family policies in the public and private sectors. Such changes will make the principles behind affirmative action more than a set of ideals to which we aspire; they will become part of the fabric of everyday life, making discrimination part of our history, not an impediment to our future.

IQ Eye Openers—The Evidence Is in: The Case for Affirmative Action

---

1. Women currently make up nearly half of the nation's workforce.[1]

    99 percent of women in the U.S. will work for pay sometime during their lives.[2]

    In 1968, on average, women left work for 10 years after their children were born; in 1987, they left for six months.[3]

2. Between 1980 and 1990, the proportion of all managers who are white women grew by about one-third, from 27 to 35 percent, while the proportion of all managers who are

women of color more than doubled, increasing from 3 to 7 percent.

In 1990, among full-time salaried managers, only 6.3 percent of white women and 3.6 percent of women of color earned incomes in the top 20 percent.[4]

In 1992, when 42 percent of all managers were women, only 13 percent of the business experts named in the *New York Times, Wall Street Journal, Fortune,* and *Business Week* were women.[5]

3. A 1995 study by Catalyst found that 68 percent of the CEOs at America's leading corporations consider recruiting female directors a top priority, and 86 percent consider increasing the number of women on their boards "important."[6]

4. As of March 31, 1995, women or people of color owned a total of 110 banks, or about 1 percent of all commercial banks. Women alone owned only .05 percent of the total.[7]

    Even under affirmative action, businesses owned by people of color or women get fewer than 6 percent of all federal contracts.[8]

    In 1980, women-owned firms received 0.8 percent of federal-contract awards over $25,000 and in 1991 the figure was 0.9 percent. In 1993, 1.8 percent of all federal-procurement awards and 1.2 percent of prime contracts went to women-owned businesses.[9]

    In 1994, the National Foundation for Women Business Owners found that the 7.7 million women-owned businesses in the U.S. employed 15.5 million people—white people, including men, and people of color—35 percent more than all Fortune 500 companies combined.[10]

5. Between 1987 and 1994, 10,501 race-based reverse-discrimination charges were filed by white men and resolved by the Equal Employment Opportunity Commission (EEOC). Of these cases, the EEOC found that only 1,072, approximately 10 percent, had merit. In 1994 alone, this number fell to a mere 0.2 percent.

    In reverse-discrimination cases filed by either women or men in 1994, the EEOC found in favor of the complainants in 13.2 percent of race-based, 12.7 percent of national origin-based, and 16.6 percent of gender-based cases.[11]

6. In 1966, two and one-half million women attended college. In 1975, three years after President Nixon signed into law Title IX of the Education Amendments Act, the number of women in college doubled to over five million. In 1979, women college students outnumbered men for the first time in U.S. history. Currently, over eight million women attend college, composing 55.1 percent of the total enrollment.[12]

According to the EEOC, college-educated women earn 29 percent less than college-educated men and make only $1,950 more per year than high-school-educated white men.[13]

7. The U.S. Department of Education estimates that only 40 cents of every $1,000 of federal-educational assistance funds minority-targeted scholarships.[14]

8. When Richmond, VA, suspended its affirmative-action programs in 1987, city contracts to minorities dropped from 41.6 percent to 2.2 percent.[15]

In Los Angeles, where non-whites make up two-thirds of the population, only 5 percent of every public-works dollar goes to minority-owned contractors.[16]

9. In the mid-1990s, white men make up 33 percent of the population. They are: 85 percent of tenured professors; 85 percent of partners in law firms; 80 percent of the U.S. House of Representatives; 90 percent of the U.S. Senate; 95 percent of Fortune 500 CEOs; 97 percent of school superintendents; 99.9 percent of athletic team owners; and 100 percent of all U.S. presidents.[17]

NOTES

Affirming Diversity:
Building a National Community that Works

1. Reginald Wilson, "Affirmative Action: Yesterday, Today, and Beyond" (Washington, DC: American Council on Education, May 1995). Photocopy.

2. Federal Glass Ceiling Commission, *Good for Business: Making full use of the nation's human capital: The environmental scan* (Washington, DC: U.S. Department of Labor, 1995). President Bush appointed the Federal Glass Ceiling Commission, a 21-member bipartisan group, under the Civil Rights Act (CRA) of 1991 after Senator Robert Dole introduced the Glass Ceiling Act, which became Title II of the CRA. The commission also plans to publish *A Strategic Plan*, which will recommend ways to dismantle artificial barriers to advancement for white women and men and women of color.

3. Federal Glass Ceiling Commission, iii–iv, 12, 13, 9.

4. Ibid., 28.

5. William B. Johnston and Arnold H. Packer, *Workforce 2000: Work and Workers for the 21st Century* (Indianapolis, IN: Hudson Institute, 1987), xx, 89.

6. A February 1994 article in *Entrepreneur* reported that diversity training workshops typically last from half a day to three days and cost companies from $500 to $5000. Jane Easter Bahls, "Culture Shock," *Entrepreneur* (Feb-ruary 1994): n.p. For a critique of "diversity management," see Avery Gordon, "The Work of Corporate Culture: Diversity Management," *Social Text* 44 vol. 13, no. 3 (Fall/Winter 1995): 3–30.

7. Equal Employment Opportunity Commission, "EEOC Charge Resolution Statistics Reflecting Type of Reverse Discrimination." Photocopy.

8. "Catalyst Fact Sheet: National Business Women's Week, October 16–20, 1995." Photocopy.

9. "Excerpts from the Decision on Justifying Affirmative Action Programs," *New York Times* (June 13, 1995): D24.

10. Louis Harris, *Women's Equality Poll, 1995* (Arlington, VA: Feminist Majority Foundation, 1995): Photocopy.

11. Peter Applebome, "The Debate on Diversity in California Shifts," *New York Times* (June 4, 1995): 22.

12. Ibid.

13. Claude M. Steele, "Black Students Live Down to Expectations," *New York Times* (August 31, 1995): A25.

14. William Cellis, "40 Years After Brown, Segregation Persists," *New York Times* (May 18, 1994): A1. And Steven A. Holmes, "Look Who's Saying Separate is Equal," *New York Times* (October 1, 1995): Sec. 4, p. 5.

15. For a report that links the glass ceiling and the sticky floor, see Sharon L. Harlan and Catherine White Berheide, *Barriers to Workplace Advancement Experienced by Women in Low-Paying Occupations* (Albany, NY: Center for Women in Government, 1994).

16. Sam Roberts, "Women's Work: What's New, What Isn't," *New York Times* (April 27, 1995): B6.

17. Coalition of Labor Union Women, "What is Affirmative Action?" Photocopy.

18. Orna Feldman, "Secretary of Labor Robert Reich: Public Policies Must Address Investment in Human Capital," *Radcliffe News* (September 1995): 2. And *1993 Handbook on Women Workers: Trends & Issues* (Washington, DC: US Department of Labor, Women's Bureau, 1994), 201.

19. US Bureau of the Census, reported by the Institute for Women's Policy Research, Washington, DC.

20. Jennifer Tucker and Leslie R. Wolfe, *Defining Work and Family Issues: Listening to the Voices of Women of Color* (Washington, DC: Center for Women Policy Studies, 1994).

Eye Openers: The Evidence Is in: The Case for Affirmative Action

1. Women's Bureau, U.S. Department of Labor, *Working Women Count! A Report to the Nation* (Washington, DC: US Department of Labor, 1994), 4.

2. Ibid.

3. Jeffrey Rosen, "Affirmative Action: A Solution," *New Republic* vol. 4, no. 190 (May 8, 1995): 20.

4. Jill Braunstein, Heidi I. Hartmann, and Lois Shaw, "Restructuring Work: How Have Women and Minority Managers Fared?" (Washington, DC: Institute for Women's Policy Research, 1995). Pamphlet.

5. Carol Wheeler, "How Much Ink Do Women Get?" *Executive Female* (September/October 1994): 51.

6. Catalyst, "CEOs Seek More Female Directors," *Perspectives* II (Spring 1995).

7. Board of Governors of the Federal Reserve System, conversation with NCRW.

8. Tamar Lewin, "Reactions: 5–4 Decision Buoys Some; For Others It's a Setback," *New York Times* (June 13, 1995): D25.

9. Women's Transportation Seminar. "Fact Sheet on Women-Owned Businesses." Photocopy.

10. Catalyst, "Catalyst Fact Sheet: National Business Women's Week. October 16–20, 1995.." Photocopy.

11. Equal Employment Opportunity Commission, "EEOC Charge Resolution Statistics Reflecting Type of Reverse Discrimination." Photocopy.

12. American Civil Liberties Union, memo (March 6, 1965). Photocopy, 3. And "The Nation," *Chronicle of Higher Education Almanac* vol. XLII, no. 1 (September 1, 1995): 5.

13. Equal Employment Opportunity Commission, "Wage Gap" Photocopy, 1.

14. *Affirmative Action Review: Report to the President* (Washington, DC: The White House, 1995), 87.

15. Californians for Equal Opportunity (June 14, 1995). E-mail.

16. American Civil Liberties Union of Southern California, "Why We Still Need Affirmative Action—A Few Statistics." Photocopy.

17. Ibid.

Perspectives

1. Michael L. Wheeler, *Diversity Training* (New York: Conference Board, 1994), 9.

Special Report: Holding the Line: Californians Seize the Initiative on Affirmative Action

1. B. Drummond Ayres Jr., "Efforts to End Job Preferences are Faltering," *New York Times* (November 20, 1995): B10.

Working Trends: Counting on the Nation's Women

1. About 18 percent of the general population lacks health insurance. These numbers are drawn from a scientifically selected, national random sample of respondents the Women's Bureau telephoned directly. The scientific sample provides a benchmark for evaluating the responses of more than 250,000 women who chose to answer a popular questionnaire distributed with the help of 1600 partners, including businesses, grassroots organizations, unions, daily newspapers, national magazines, and federal agencies in 1994. Women's Bureau, *Working Women Count! A Report to the Nation* (Washington, DC: US Department of Labor, 1994), 6–7.

2. U.S. Department of Labor, "Working Women Count Recommendations: Making Work Better for Women" (Washington, DC: U.S. Department of Labor, March 15, 1995).

Policy in Action: We Are Family

1. In addition, to be eligible, employees must have worked for the employer for at least 12 months and for 1250 hours during the year preceding the leave. FMLA requires employers to maintain an employee's health benefits during the leave, and they may not require employees to forfeit any previously accrued seniority or benefits as a result of the leave. However, employers are not required to count the leave time as time accrued for purposes of seniority or other benefits.

2. Young-Hee Yoon, Heidi Hartmann, and Jill Braunstein, "Using Temporary Disability Insurance to Provide Paid Family Leave: A Comparison with the Family Medical Leave Act," (Washington, DC: Institute for Women's Policy Research, 1995). Pamphlet, 1.

3. Mike Meyers, "Taking Pregnancy Leaves," *Star Tribune* (February 6, 1995).

4. Julianne O'Gara, *Making Workplaces Work: Quality Work Policies for Small Business* (Washington, DC: Business and Professional Women's Foundation, 1995), 22.

5. Jeffrey Goldfarb, "Employment: Majority of U.S. Workers are Unaware of FMLA Provisions, BNA Survey Finds," *Analysis and Reports* (Washington, DC: Bureau of National Affairs, 1994), C1.

6. Commission on Family and Medical Leave, "New Studies Measure Impact of Family & Medical Leave Law" (Washington, DC: U.S. Department of Labor, 1995). Photocopy.

7. Katherine A. McGonagle et al., "Commission on Leave Survey of Employees on the Impact of the Family and Medical Leave Act." (Ann Arbor, MI: Institute for Social Research, 1995): Photocopy, 23. See also, David Cantor et al., "The Impact of the Family and Medical Leave Act: A Survey of Employers" (Rockville, MD: Westat, 1995). Photocopy.

8. Yoon, Harmann, and Braunstein, 4.

9. Ibid., Table 2.

Girls Report: Minding Her Own Business: Girls Invest in Their Futures

1. "Camp $tart-Up Takes Off," *Future Perfect* (Fall 1995): 3.

QUESTIONS

1. Fairness and the meaning of equality are basic questions behind affirmative action. If we do not begin life with a "level playing field," do we ensure equal opportunity to all who are promised it? Why is affirmative action "affirmative"?

2. What are two sources of discrimination? Do you think discrimination occurs because of individual intent, or is it institutional? What individual attributes might be responsible for racial/sexual discrimination? Who should be held accountable when institutions discriminate?

3. Childcare is usually considered apart from affirmative action. However, women's over-responsibility for "family matters" places an unequal burden of care on them. How could society ensure this does not unfairly disadvantage women at work or school?

Feminism and
Women's Movements

Susan M. Hartmann

Women in the United States have engaged in political activism on behalf of their rights and interests as women for more than 150 years. These movements have included women from diverse walks of life, social classes, regions, races and nationalities, and political and religious groups. The overall goal of these movements has been toward improving women's position in society, but the focus and priorities have changed greatly over a century and a half.

In the early 19th century women had no right to vote and limited opportunities for education. Married women had no right to their own earnings, to hold property of their own, to divorce, except in extreme cases, or to retain custody of their children. Securing such fundamental rights became the focus of early feminists. As women achieved some of their goals, concerns turned to other issues, such as the right to equal pay for equal work, to control reproduction, and to eliminate violence against women.

The terms "feminist" and "feminism" did not come into existence in the United States until the early 20th century. What it means to be a "feminist" has been and continues to be a subject of debate and confusion. One useful and simple way to define feminism is: "a recognition and critique of male supremacy combined with efforts to change it." Such a definition allows us to use the term to discuss activism that occurred before the term came into use and to refer to movements that might not have borne that label.

A form of activism that would eventually come to be called "womanism" developed in the context of the African-American racial uplift movement. "Womanism," a term coined by Alice Walker in 1983, places feminist concerns as a part of African-American struggles for self-determination and equality and stresses black women's ties with men in their racial community.

Although womanism and feminism have existed in the United States since the 1830s, especially significant developments have taken place during three periods: (1) the 1830s through the 1860s; (2) the 1890s to 1920; and (3) the 1960s and beyond.

The first women's rights movement grew in part out of women's experiences in reform movements such as temperance and abolition. Among the women and men who gathered in Seneca Falls, New York in 1848 to issue the first collective call for women's rights, many had worked in the movement to eliminate slavery, and the women's rights movement remained linked to the abolitionist movement until the 1860s. The early women's movement gained some rights for married women and helped push open some doors to higher education, but the voting booth remained closed to women.

The struggle for suffrage took center stage during the years from 1890 to 1920. In the late 19th century, black and white women began to organize in large numbers, forming clubs for self-improvement and working to improve conditions in their communities; and many women came to the suffrage movement through these reform activities. Although women could vote in a handful of states by 1910, suffragists struggled and failed dozens of times to get state legislatures to act on their behalf. After 1910, they increasingly focused on the national level and an amendment to the federal Constitution.

Suffragists were overwhelmingly native-born, white, and middle-class, and they sometimes used racist and anti-immigrant arguments to advance their cause. Racist attitudes and the desire to win Southern support for suffrage also led white suffrage leaders to rebuff black women who were eager to work for the ballot, but African American women launched a large effort on their own.

During the 1910s suffragists stepped up their activism, involving some two million women to the cause, engaging in lobbying, door-to-door canvassing, huge parades, and other public demonstrations. One group of suffragists picketed the White House and served time in jail when they resisted police orders to disperse. The nation's entrance into World War I in 1917 helped the cause by highlighting women's contributions to the public sphere and exposing the country's failure to live up to its ideal of representative government. This along with the militant tactics that gained publicity for suffrage and the decades of organizing that had begun in 1848 won Congressional approval of the 19th amendment in 1919 and ratification in 1920.

Women continued to organize after winning the vote, pursuing such goals as equal pay, birth control, and the right to serve on juries, but they did so in much smaller numbers. Not until the 1960s did another grass-roots movement arise to rival the suffrage movement. Spurred in part by the civil rights movement and the moral climate it created, multitudes of women launched a revolution that attacked sex discrimination and sought a greater presence and influence for women in the public sphere, control over reproduction, and dramatic changes in social norms about how women could and should live their lives. They introduced entirely new issues into the public policy agenda, including those dealing with sexuality, reproduction, and violence against women.

Targets of feminist and womanist protest included traditional religion, pornography, the treatment of women in the welfare system, images of women in mass media, discrimination against lesbians, and involuntary sterilization of poor and minority women. The broad range of feminist issues mirrored the tremendous diversity among women as women of color, lesbians, and working-class women challenged white, middle-class feminists, who tended to be the public spokespersons for the women's movement, to look beyond their own immediate interests. The existence of feminist and womanist aspirations among such diverse groups of women ensured the survival of activism through the end of the twentieth century. Indeed, feminist and womanist concerns have made inroads in many mainstream institutions and organizations such as labor unions, organized religion, professional associations, the military, the United Nations, athletics, and universities. Feminists participate in and influence other social movements and protest organizations concerned with civil rights,

43

gay and lesbian issues, homelessness, AIDS activism, environmental concerns and human rights.

The landscape of contemporary feminism for younger women is increasingly influenced by popular culture, by new forms of technology, and by the growth of women's studies. Women's agency and feminist themes are celebrated in rap, rock and alternative forms of music. In 1997, Lilith Fair, a musical extravaganza featuring female artists and feminist activists, played to sell-out crowds across the U.S. and Canada. Female rappers with feminist sensibilities adorn the cover of popular magazines and are demanding more artistic freedom within the industry.

Feminism can be found in cyberspace where technology is used as an international organizing tool to bring women from around the world together. Information can be shared in newer and quicker forms reducing the isolation of activists in different parts of the world who are working on similar issues. Women in different parts of the U.S. can also communicate with each other through chat rooms and special interest news groups. Feminist organizations are publishing on-line magazines and journals concerning women's issues and creating informative web sites about women's social, economic and political status.

Women's studies courses, now found in over 600 universities and colleges, introduce students to feminist ideas and to the history of women's movements. Students in a variety of majors take women's studies courses as part of their general education. Graduates of women's studies programs are working in government, in industry and in the growing non-profit sector to improve the status of women in a range of programs—from violence prevention efforts, to women's health initiatives, to training women for employment in the skilled trades.

Women's goals and activism have changed over the past two centuries. While there have been many successes much remains on the political agenda. More women are doctors, lawyers and business owners at the same time as more women are living in poverty. Because of the writing, theorizing and activism of diverse groups of women—lesbians, poor and working class women, women of color, and women with disabilities—we are more aware of the diversity of women's experiences. We are also more aware of the need for multiple forms of feminism to inspire and frame our understanding of women's issues and activism at home and abroad.

FURTHER READINGS

Linda M. Blum, *Between Feminism and Labor: the Significance of the Comparable Worth Movement* (Berkeley: University of California Press, 1991).

Flora Davis, *Moving the Mountain: The Woman's Movement in America Since 1960* (New York: Simon and Schuster, 1991).

Sara Evans, *Personal Politics: The Roots of Women's Liberation in the Civil Rights Movement and the New Left* (New York: Vintage, 1979).

Eleanor Flexner, *Century of Struggle: The Women's Movement in the United States* (Cambridge: Belknap Press of Harvard University, rev. ed. 1996).

Paula Giddings, *When and Where I Enter: The Impact of Black Women on Race and Sex in America* (New York: Bantam, 1984).

Susan M. Hartmann, *From Margin to Mainstream: American Women and Politics Since the 1960s* (New York: Knopf, 1989).

Leila Rupp and Verta Taylor, *Survival in the Doldrums: The American Women's Rights Movement, 1945 to the 1960s* (New York: Oxford University Press, 1987).

Verta Taylor, *Rock-a-by Baby: Feminism, Self-Help, and Postpartum Depression* (New York: Routledge, 1996).

Nancy Whittier, *Feminist Generations: The Persistence of the Radical Women's Movement* (Philadelphia: Temple University Press, 1995).

IS EQUALITY INDIGENOUS?
THE UNTOLD IROQUOIS INFLUENCE
ON EARLY RADICAL FEMINISTS
(1996)

Sally Roesch Wagner

Although feminist scholars generally agree that the 1848 Seneca Falls Convention marked the beginning of the women's movement in the United States, many examples of women's dissatisfaction and activism precede this catalytic event. In the following article, Sally Roesch Wagner, an historian, adds further insight into the factors giving rise to the early movement by considering how Iroquois women's cultural beliefs and practices influenced the vision of early feminist leaders.

I had been haunted by a question to the past, a mystery of feminist history: *How did the radical suffragists come to their vision, a vision not of Band-Aid reform but of a reconstituted world completely transformed?*

For 20 years I had immersed myself in the writings of early United States women's rights activists—Matilda Joslyn Gage (1826–1898), Elizabeth Cady Stanton (1815–1902), Lucretia Mott (1793–1880)—yet I could not fathom how they dared to dream their revolutionary dream. Living under the ideological hegemony of nineteenth-century United States, they had no say in government, religion, economics, or social life ("the four-fold oppression" of their lives, Gage and Stanton called it). *Whatever made them think that human harmony—based on the perfect equality of all people, with women absolute sovereigns of their lives—was an achievable goal?*

Surely these white women, living under conditions of virtual slavery, did not get their vision in a vacuum. Somehow they were able to see from point A, where they stood—corseted, ornamental, legally nonpersons—to point C, the "regenerated" world Gage predicted, in which all repressive institutions would be destroyed. What was point B in their lives, the earthly alternative that drove their feminist spirit—not a utopian pipe dream but a sensible, doable paradigm?

Then I realized I had been skimming over the source of their inspiration without noticing it. My own unconscious white supremacy had kept me from recognizing what these prototypical feminists kept insisting in their writings: They caught a glimpse of the possibility of freedom because they knew women who lived liberated lives, women who had always possessed rights beyond their wildest imagination—Iroquois women.

The more evidence I uncovered of this indelible Native American influence on the vision of early United States feminists, the more certain I became that this story must be told.

A Vision of Everyday Decency

It is difficult for white Americans today to picture the extended period in history when—before the United States government's Indian-reservation system, like apartheid, concretized a separation of the races in the last half of the nineteenth century—regular trade, cultural sharing, even friendship between Native Americans and Euro-Americans was common. Perhaps nowhere was this now-lost social ease more evident than in the towns and

villages in upstate New York where Elizabeth Cady Stanton and
Matilda Joslyn Gage lived and Lucretia Mott visited. All three
suffragists personally knew Iroquois women, citizens of the six-
nation confederacy (Seneca, Cayuga, Onondaga, Oneida,
Mohawk, and later Tuscarora) that had established peace among
themselves before Columbus came to this "old" world.

Stanton, for instance, sat across the dinner table from Oneida
women during her frequent visits to her cousin, the radical social
activist Gerrit Smith, in Peterboro. Smith's daughter, also named
Elizabeth, was first to shed the 20 pounds of clothing that fashion
dictated should hang from a white woman's waist, dangerously
deformed from corseting. The reform costume Elizabeth Smith
adopted (named the "Bloomer" after the newspaper editor who
popularized it) bore an uncanny resemblance to the loose-fitting
tunic and leggings worn by the two Elizabeths' Native American
friends.

Gage, appointed by a women's rights convention in the 1850s,
worked on a committee with *New York Tribune* editor Horace
Greeley to document the woefully few jobs open to white women.
Meanwhile she knew hardy, nearby Onondaga women who
farmed corn, beans, and squash—nutritionally balanced and eco-
logically near-perfect crops called the Three Sisters by the
Haudenosaunee (traditional Iroquois).

Lucretia Mott and her husband, James, were members of the
Indian Committee of the Philadelphia Yearly Meeting of the Society of Friends. For years this committee of Quakers befriended the
Seneca, setting up a school and model farm at Cattaraugus and
helping them save some of their territory from unscrupulous land
speculators. In the summer of 1848 Mott spent a month at
Cattaraugus witnessing women share in discussion and decision-
making as the Seneca nation reorganized their governmental
structure. Her feminist vision fired by that experience, Mott trav-
eled that July from the Seneca nation to nearby Seneca Falls,
where she and Stanton held the world's first women's rights
convention.

Stanton, Gage, and Mott regularly read newspaper accounts
of everyday Iroquois activities—a recent condolence ceremony (to
mourn a chief's death and to set in place a new one); the latest
sports scores (a lacrosse match between the Mohawk and the
Onondaga); a Quaker council called to ask Seneca women to leave
their fields and work in the home (as the Friends said God com-

manded but as Mott opposed). Stanton, Gage, and Mott could also read that according to interviews with white teachers at various Indian nations, Indian men did not rape women. Front-page stories admonished big-city dandies to learn a thing or two from Indian men's example, so that white women too could walk around any time of the day or night without fear.

In the United States, until women's rights advocates began the painstaking task of changing state laws, a husband had the legal right to batter his wife (to interfere would "upset the domestic tranquillity of the home," one state supreme court held). But suffragists lived as neighbors to men of other nations whose religious, legal, social, and economic concept of women made such behavior unthinkable. Haudenosaunee spiritual practices were spelled out in an oral tradition called the Code of Handsome Lake, which told this cautionary tale (as reported by a white woman who was a contemporary of Stanton and Gage) of what would befall batterers in the afterlife:

> [A man] who was in the habit of beating his wife, was led to the red-hot statue of a female, and requested to treat it as he had done his wife. He commenced beating it, and the sparks flew out and were continually burning him. Thus would it be done to all who beat their wives.

To Stanton, Gage, Mott, and their feminist contemporaries, the Native American conception of everyday decency, nonviolence, and gender justice must have seemed the promised land.

A Vision of Power and Security

As a feminist historian, I did not at first pay attention to such references to American Indian life because I believed what I had been taught: that Native American women were poor, downtrodden "beasts of burden" (as they were often called in the nineteenth century). I did not know what I was looking for, so of course I could not see it.

I remembered that in the early 1970s, some feminist historians flirted with the idea of prehistoric matriarchies on which to pin women's egalitarian hopes. Anthropologists soon set us straight about such nonsense. The evidence just wasn't there, they said. But Paula Gunn Allen, a Laguna Pueblo/Sioux author and scholar, believed otherwise. "Before we decide," she wrote in 1981,

> that belief in ancient matriarchal civilization is an irratio-
> nal concept born of conjecture and wish, let us adjust our
> perspective to match that of our foresisters. Then, when
> we search the memories and lore of tribal peoples, we
> might be able to see what eons and all kinds of institutions
> have conspired to hide from our eyes. . . . The evidence is
> all around us. It remains for us to discover what it means.

Allen's words opened my eyes, threw into question everything I thought I knew about the nineteenth-century women's
movement, and sent me on a wholly new course of historical
discovery. The results shook the foundation of the feminist theory
I had been teaching for almost 20 years.

About eight years ago, early in my new phase of research, I sat
in the kitchen of Alice Papineau-Dewasenta, an Onondaga clan
mother. Over iced tea, Alice described to me the unbroken custom
by which traditional Iroquois (Haudenosaunee) clan mothers
nominate the male chiefs who go on to represent their clans in the
Grand Council. She listed the qualifications: "First, they cannot
have committed a theft. Second, they cannot have committed a
murder. Third, they cannot have sexually assaulted a woman."

There goes Congress! I thought to myself. Then a wishful fantasy occurred: What if only women in the United States chose
governmental representatives and, like Haudenosaunee women,
alone had the right "to knock the horns off the head," as Stanton
marveled—to oust officials if they failed to represent the needs of
the people unto the seventh generation?

If I am so inspired by Alice's words to dream today, imagine
how the founding feminists felt as they beheld the Iroquois world.
For instance, shortly after Matilda Joslyn Gage was arrested in
1893 at her home in New York for the "crime" of trying to vote in
a school board election, she was adopted into the Wolf clan of the
Mohawk nation and given the name Karonienhawi (Sky Carrier).
In the Mohawk nation, women alone had the authority to nominate the chief, after counseling with all the people of the clan.
What must it have meant to Gage to know of such real-life political power?

And Elizabeth Cady Stanton—called a heretic and worse for
advocating divorce laws that would allow women to leave love-
less and dangerous marriages—admired the model of divorce

Iroquois-style: "No matter how many children or whatever goods he might have in the house," Stanton informed the National Council of Women convention in 1891, the "luckless husband or lover who was too shiftless to do his share of the providing" in an Iroquois marriage "might at any time be ordered to pick up his blanket and budge; and after such an order it would not be healthful for him to attempt to disobey." What must it have meant to Stanton to know of such real-life domestic security?

A Vision of Radical Respect

While early women's rights activists began to be successful in changing some repressive laws, an ensuing backlash in the 1870s resulted in the criminalization of birth control and family planning, and child custody remained the right of fathers. How, then, did Stanton and her daughter Harriot envision "voluntary motherhood"—a revolutionary alternative to the patriarchal family, with women controlling their own bodies and having rights to the children they bore? Well, a short distance from the Stanton home in Seneca Falls, the Seneca women practiced it.

Among the Haudenosaunee, family lineage was reckoned through mothers; no child was born a "bastard" (the concept didn't exist); every child found a loving and welcome place in a mother's world, surrounded by a mother's sisters, her mother, and the men whom they married. Unmarried sons and brothers lived in this large extended family, too, until they left home to marry into another matrilocal clan. Stanton envied how American Indian women "ruled the house" and how "descent of property and children were in the female line." Gage, while serving as president of the National Woman Suffrage Association in 1875, penned a series of admiring articles about the Iroquois for the New York *Evening Post* in which she wrote that the "division of power between the sexes in this Indian republic was nearly equal" while the Iroquois family structure "demonstrated woman's superiority in power." For these white women living in a world where marital rape was commonplace and forbidden by neither church nor state (although the Comstock Laws of the 1870s outlawed discussion of it), Indian women's violence-free and empowered home life must have looked like heaven.

It wasn't simply that Euro-American women had no rights;

once they married they had no legal existence. "The two shall become one and the one is the man," preached Christianity. This canon (church) law had been turned into common law, according to which married women were legally dead; therefore married women could not have custody of their children or rights to their own property or earnings, sign contracts, sue or be sued, or vote.

Until women's rights advocates began to change divorce laws in the last half of the nineteenth century, divorce was not allowed by church or state. Women fleeing from a violent husband could be returned to him by the police, as runaway slaves were returned to their master. Husbands, before they died, could will away an unborn child, and after its father's death the baby would be taken from its mother and given to its "rightful owner." And until the Married Women's Property Acts were slowly enacted state by state throughout the nineteenth century, any money a wife earned or inherited belonged outright to her husband.

A married woman was "nameless, purseless and childless," Stanton summed up, though she be "a woman, heiress and mother." Calling for an end to this injustice, the early suffragists were labeled hopeless dreamers for imagining a world so clearly against nature, and worse, heretics for daring to question God's divine plan.

From her firsthand knowledge of the Iroquois, Stanton knew that the patriarchal "women's sphere" was not universal. When called a "savage," for instance, for practicing natural childbirth, Stanton rebutted her critics by mocking their use of the word; she also pointed out that Indian women "do not suffer" giving birth— thus it was absurd to suppose "that only enlightened Christian women are cursed" by painful, difficult childbirth. Stanton, whose major work, *The Woman's Bible,* was published in 1895, became convinced that the oppression of women was not divinely inspired at all. "The Bible," she wrote,

> makes woman a mere after thought in creation; the author of evil; cursed in her maternity; a subject in marriage; and claims divine authority for this fourfold bondage, this wholesale disecration of the mothers of the race. I do not believe God ever wrote or inspired such sentiments.

Gage agreed, naming the church the "bulwark" of women's oppression. "In the name of religion," Gage wrote in *Woman,*

Church and State, published in 1893, "the worst crimes against humanity have ever been perpetrated."

In the 1890s, when the religious right tried to destroy religious freedom by placing God in the Constitution and prayer in public schools and by pushing a conservative political agenda, Stanton and Gage (Mott had died) determined to challenge the church. Their theory held that women in indigenous cultures had respect and authority in egalitarian and women-centered societies that worshipped a female deity. This matriarchal system was over-thrown, Stanton contended, when "Christianity putting the religious weapon into man's hand made his conquest complete."

A common myth held that Christianity and civilization meant progress for women, but Stanton and Gage saw through it. At the 1888 International Council of Women, they listened as Alice Fletcher, a noted white ethnographer, spoke about the greater rights of American Indian women. Fletcher made clear that these Indian women were well aware that when they became United States citizens, they would lose their rights. Fletcher quoted one who told her:

> As an Indian woman I was free. I owned my home, my person, the work of my own hands, and my children could never forget me. I was better as an Indian woman than under white law.

Fletcher also quoted an Indian man who reproached white men: "Your laws show how little your men care for their women. The wife is nothing of herself." He was not alone in chastising white men for their domination of women. A Tuscarora chief, Elias Johnson, writing about the absence of rape among Iroquois men in his popular 1881 book, *Legends, Traditions and Laws, of the Iroquois, or Six Nations . . . ,* commented wryly that European men had held the same respect for women "until they became civilized." According to a New York paper, a Cayuga chief, Dr. Peter Wilson, addressing the New York Historical Society in 1866, encouraged white men to use the occasion of Southern reconstruction to establish universal suffrage, "even of the women, as in his nation." Today, try as I might, I cannot begin to imagine how such Iroquois men's radical respect for women's lives must have sounded to early feminists' ears.

A Vision of Responsibilities

A few years ago I was invited to lecture at the annual Elizabeth Cady Stanton birthday tea in Seneca Falls with Audry Shenandoah, an Onondaga nation clan mother. A crowd of my feminist contemporaries packed the elegant, century-old hotel, and I spoke of my deep gratitude for the profound influence of the Iroquois on early feminists' vision of women's rights.

Then Audry talked matter-of-factly about the responsibilities of Haudenosaunee women in their system of gender balance: Iroquois women continue to have the responsibility of nominating, counseling, and keeping in office the male chief who represents the clan in the Grand Council. In the six nations of the Iroquois confederacy, she explained, Haudenosaunee women have worked with the men to successfully guard their sovereign political status against persistent attempts to turn them into United States citizens. In Audry's direct and simple telling, the social power of the Haudenosaunee women seemed almost unremarkable—"We have always had these responsibilities," she said. I caught my breath again, remembering that radical suffragists also knew such women who lived their vision.

My feminist terminology had revealed my cultural bias. Out of habit I had referred to women's empowerment as women's "rights." But for Iroquois women who have maintained many of their traditional ways despite two centuries of white Americans' attempts to "civilize and Christianize" them, the concept of women's "rights" actually has little meaning. To the Haudenosaunee, it is simply their way of life. Their egalitarian relationships and their political authority are a reality that—like my foresisters—I still but dream.

QUESTIONS

1. According to Wagner, how did Iroquois women influence the leaders of the early women's movement? What relationship did Iroquois women have with early feminists? What examples does she offer?

2. How did the rights of Iroquois and Anglo-American women differ in the nineteenth century? How did this affect early leaders? What "visions" does Wagner discuss? What was significant about the Iroquois vision of "voluntary mother-hood"?

3. How does this article alter your understanding of the origins of the women's movement? What significance does it have for thinking about women's history?

DECLARATION OF SENTIMENTS AND RESOLUTIONS (1848)

The Seneca Falls Women's Rights Convention of 1848

This document, drawn in 1848, was a product of the first meeting on women's rights in the United States. Written in a style similar to the Declaration of Independence, *the document presents the many injustices women faced in the nineteenth century. From a contemporary viewpoint, the document provides important historical information on the origins of social movements seeking improvement in the quality of women's lives.*

When, in the course of human events, it becomes necessary for one portion of the family of man to assume among the people of the earth a position different from that which they have hitherto occupied, but one to which the laws of nature and of nature's God entitle them, a decent respect to the opinions of mankind requires that they should declare the causes that impel them to such a course.

"Declaration of Sentiments and Resolutions," from The Seneca Falls Women's Rights Convention of 1848.

We hold these truths to be self-evident: that all men and women are created equal; that they are endowed by their Creator with certain inalienable rights; that among these are life, liberty, and the pursuit of happiness; that to secure these rights governments are instituted, deriving their just powers from the consent of the governed. Whenever any form of government becomes destructive of these ends, it is the right of those who suffer from it to refuse allegiance to it, and to insist upon the institution of a new government, laying its foundation on such principles, and organizing its powers in such form, as to them shall seem most likely to effect their safety and happiness. Prudence, indeed, will dictate that governments long established should not be changed for light and transient causes; and accordingly all experience hath shown that mankind are more disposed to suffer, while evils are sufferable, than to right themselves by abolishing the forms to which they were accustomed. But when a long train of abuses and usurpations, pursuing invariably the same object evinces a design to reduce them under absolute despotism, it is their duty to throw off such government, and to provide new guards for their future security. Such has been the patient sufferance of the women under this government, and such is now the necessity which constrains them to demand the equal station to which they are entitled.

The history of mankind is a history of repeated injuries and usurpations on the part of man toward woman, having in direct object the establishment of an absolute tyranny over her. To prove this, let facts be submitted to a candid world.

He has never permitted her to exercise her inalienable right to the elective franchise.

He has compelled her to submit to laws, in the formation of which she had no voice.

He has withheld from her rights which are given to the most ignorant and degraded men—both natives and foreigners.

Having deprived her of this first right of a citizen, the elective franchise, thereby leaving her without representation in the halls of legislation, he has oppressed her on all sides.

He has made her, if married, in the eye of the law, civilly dead.

He has taken from her all right in property, even to the wages she earns.

He has made her, morally, an irresponsible being, as she can commit many crimes with impunity, provided they be done in the presence of her husband. In the covenant of marriage, she is compelled to promise obedience to her husband, he becoming, to all intents and purposes, her master—the law giving him power to deprive her of her liberty, and to administer chastisement.

He has so framed the laws of divorce, as to what shall be the proper causes, and in case of separation, to whom the guardianship of the children shall be given, as to be wholly regardless of the happiness of women—the law, in all cases, going upon a false supposition of the supremacy of man, and giving all power into his hands.

After depriving her of all rights as a married woman, if single, and the owner of property, he has taxed her to support a government which recognizes her only when her property can be made profitable to it.

He has monopolized nearly all the profitable employments, and from those she is permitted to follow, she receives but a scanty remuneration. He closes against her all the avenues to wealth and distinction which he considers most honorable to himself. As a teacher of theology, medicine, or law, she is not known.

He has denied her the facilities for obtaining a thorough education, all colleges being closed against her.

He allows her in Church, as well as State, but a subordinate position, claiming Apostolic authority for her exclusion from the ministry, and, with some exceptions, from any public participation in the affairs of the Church.

He has created a false public sentiment by giving to the world a different code of morals for men and women, by which moral delinquencies which exclude women from society, are not only tolerated, but deemed of little account in man.

He has usurped the prerogative of Jehovah himself, claiming it as his right to assign for her a sphere of action, when that belongs to her conscience and to her God.

He has endeavored, in every way that he could, to destroy her confidence in her own powers, to lessen her self-respect, and to make her willing to lead a dependent and abject life.

Now, in view of this entire disfranchisement of one-half the people of this country, their social and religious degradation—in view of the unjust laws above mentioned, and because women do feel themselves aggrieved, oppressed, and fraudulently deprived of their most sacred rights, we insist that they have immediate admission to all the rights and privileges which belong to them as citizens of the United States.

In entering upon the great work before us, we anticipate no small amount of misconception, misrepresentation, and ridicule; but we shall use every instrumentality within our power to effect our object. We shall employ agents, circulate tracts, petition the State and National legislatures, and endeavor to enlist the pulpit and the press in our behalf. We hope this Convention will be followed by a series of Conventions embracing every part of the country.

Resolutions

WHEREAS, The great precept of nature is conceded to be, that "man shall pursue his own true and substantial happiness." Blackstone in his Commentaries remarks, that this law of Nature being coeval with mankind, and dictated by God himself, is of course superior in obligation to any other. It is binding over all the globe, in all countries and at all times; no human laws are of any validity if contrary to this, and such of them as are valid, derive all their force, and all their validity, and all their authority, mediately and immediately, from this original; therefore,

Resolved, That such laws as conflict, in any way, with the true and substantial happiness of woman, are contrary to the great precept of nature and of no validity, for this is "superior in obligation to any other."

Resolved, That all laws which prevent woman from occupying such a station in society as her conscience shall dictate, or which place her in a position inferior to that of man, are contrary to the great precept of nature, and therefore of no force or authority.

Resolved, That woman is man's equal—was intended to be so by the Creator, and the highest good of the race demands that she should be recognized as such.

Resolved, That the women of this country ought to be enlightened in regard to the laws under which they live, that they may no longer publish their degradation by declaring themselves satisfied with their present position, nor their ignorance, by asserting that they have all the rights they want.

Resolved, That inasmuch as man, while claiming for himself intellectual superiority, does accord to woman moral superiority, it is pre-eminently his duty to encourage her to speak and teach, as she has an opportunity, in all religious assemblies.

Resolved, That the same amount of virtue, delicacy, and refinement of behavior that is required of woman in the social state, should also be required of man, and the same transgressions should be visited with equal severity on both man and woman.

Resolved, That the objection of indelicacy and impropriety, which is so often brought against woman when she addresses a public audience, comes with a very ill-grace from those who encourage, by their attendance, her appearance on the stage, in the concert, or in feats of the circus.

Resolved, That woman has too long rested satisfied in the circumscribed limits which corrupt customs and a perverted application of the Scriptures have marked out for her, and that it is time she should move in the enlarged sphere which her great Creator has assigned her.

Resolved, That it is the duty of the women of this country to secure to themselves their sacred right to the elective franchise.

Resolved, That the equality of human rights results necessarily from the fact of the identity of the race in capabilities and responsibilities.

Resolved, therefore, That, being invested by the Creator with the same capabilities, and the same consciousness of responsibility for their exercise, it is demonstrably the right and duty of woman, equally with man, to promote every righteous cause by every righteous means; and especially in regard to the great subjects of morals and religion, it is self-evidently her right to participate with her brother in teaching them, both in private and in public, by writing and by speaking, by any instrumentalities proper to be used, and in any assemblies proper to be held; and this being a self-evident truth growing out of the divinely implanted principles of human nature, any custom or authority adverse to it, whether modern or wearing the hoary sanction of antiquity, is to be regarded as a self-evident falsehood, and at war with mankind.

[At the last session Lucretia Mott offered and spoke to the following resolution:]

Resolved, That the speedy success of our cause depends upon the zealous and untiring efforts of both men and women, for the overthrow of the monopoly of the pulpit, and for the securing to woman an equal participation with men in the various trades, professions, and commerce.

QUESTIONS

1. Explain the significance of the author's decision to use the same format as the Declaration of Independence in this document. What might this choice of format have accomplished for women in a nineteenth century context? What were the goals of the authors? What might have been the response to the document?

2. What echoes from the Seneca Falls document do you hear in contemporary feminist concerns? What contemporary concerns were not relevant for inclusion in the document at that time? What social changes might account for both the echoes and the emergence of other concerns today?

3. Who does "women" refer to in this document? What language from the text leads you to these conclusions?

4. Why is this an important document in the history of the women's movement?

"WOMANIST" FROM *IN SEARCH OF OUR MOTHERS' GARDENS* (1983)

Alice Walker

Alice Walker is an activist, a poet, and a Pulitzer Prize winning novelist. Born in Georgia in 1944, Walker attended Sarah Lawrence College, and began publishing poetry after she became active in both the voter registration movement and the welfare rights movement in the 1960s. She has published numerous novels over the course of her career, including The Third Life of Grange Copeland *(1970),* In Love and Trouble *(1973),* Meridian *(1976),* The Color Purple *(1982),* In the Temple of My Familiar *(1989),* Possessing the Secret of Joy *(1992) and* Warrior Marks *(1995).*

Since Walker's coining of the term "womanist," womanism has evolved into an academic, political and spiritual framework. The following selection presents her definition of "womanist," capturing the unique-

ness and importance of Black feminism in the United States.

Womanist 1. From *womanish*. (Opp. of "girlish," i.e., frivolous, irresponsible, not serious.) A black feminist or feminist of color. From the black folk expression of mothers to female children, "You acting womanish," i.e., like a woman. Usually referring to outrageous, audacious, courageous or *willful* behavior. Wanting to know more and in greater depth than is considered "good" for one. Interested in grown-up doings. Acting grown up. Being grown up. Interchangeable with another black folk expression: "You trying to be grown." Responsible. In charge. *Serious.*

2. *Also*: A woman who loves other women, sexually and/or nonsexually. Appreciates and prefers women's culture, women's emotional flexibility (values tears as natural counterbalance of laughter), and women's strength. Sometimes loves individual men, sexually and/or nonsexually. Committed to survival and wholeness of entire people, male *and* female. Not a separatist, except periodically, for health. Traditionally universalist as in: "Mama, why are we brown, pink, and yellow, and our cousins are white, beige, and black?" Ans.: "Well, you know the colored race is just like a flower garden, with every color flower represented." Traditionally capable, as in: "Mama, I'm walking to Canada and I'm taking you and a bunch of other slaves with me." Reply: "It wouldn't be the first time."

3. Loves music. Loves dance. Loves the moon. *Loves* the Spirit. Loves love and food and roundness. Loves struggle. *Loves* the Folk. Loves herself. *Regardless.*

4. Womanist is to feminist as purple to lavender.

QUESTIONS

---

1. What is the significance of the final line of Walker's definition? How does Walker distinguish a womanist and a feminist? What evidence from the definition can you offer to support your interpretation?

2. What is significant about the format Walker has chosen for this presentation of the definition womanist? Why?

LESBIAN VISIBILITY AND
SEXUAL RIGHTS AT BEIJING
(1996)

Ara Wilson

In 1996, the 4th World Conference on women was held in Beijing, China. A host of issues affecting women internationally were discussed, including lesbian rights. In the following essay from Signs, *Ara Wilson, an anthropologist and assistant professor of women's studies at* The Ohio State University, *discusses the unprecedented acceptance of lesbian issues she witnessed at the conference.*

As one of the more prominent and controversial topics at the Fourth World Conference on Women, lesbian issues also garnered a great deal of publicity locally in China. Rumors had prepared the Beijing police and public for a lesbian bare-breasted public demonstration, and then the rumors evolved into worldwide news when a journalist earnestly filed the erroneous report over a wire service. Even though much of the attention to lesbians at Beijing was sensationalist or hostile, it was *visibility* that was

"Lesbian Visibility and Sexual Rights at Beijing," by Ara Wilson, reprinted from *Signs*, Autumn 1996, Vol. 21, No. 1. Reprinted with permission of The University of Chicago Press. Copyright © 1996 The University of Chicago.

precisely what the lesbian organizers were after: recognition that women who love women exist in every region of the world and that the difficulties they face are serious and integral to struggles for women's equality. By and large, the efforts to work lesbian visibility into the political project at the Beijing meetings succeeded.

The organizing for lesbian participation at the Beijing meetings was located internationally in a global women's movement. It emerged from the transnational lesbian organizing that began with the UN Decade for Women, when discussions at international meetings helped cultivate lesbian organizing in Latin America and Asia in particular, networks that in turn initiated the planning for Beijing. Anjana Suwarnananda, a founder of the sole lesbian group in Thailand and one of the initiators of the Asian Lesbian Network, first proposed a lesbian space to the Non-Governmental Organization (NGO) Forum. Representatives from every region of the world worked in a network to plan for Beijing, while the U.S.-based organization, the International Gay and Lesbian Human Rights Commission (IGLHRC), served as the hub.

The lesbian issue had few full-time activists devoted to it. The majority of lesbian participants have primary commitments to other NGO work and women's groups. This cross-cause organizing has shaped the definition of lesbian issues as part of a broader international program for women's rights and development—a program to address the problems faced by women who do not wish to marry a man, who behave in ways considered unfeminine, or who love women. Even though this vision includes many women who are not properly represented by the Western term *lesbian*, notably bisexuals or, in some cultures, unmarried heterosexual women, the word prevailed as the convenient, although admittedly problematic, shorthand in most Beijing events.

The "lesbian tent," as it came to be called, lay past the McDonald's stall and the Internet center as one of the seven "diversity tents." The tent served as the place to meet, to hold workshops, to provide information, and to prepare lobbying strategies for the UN conference. The tent was intended to be inclusive of supporters, the curious, and anyone who needed shelter from the rain. But the existence of this tent was especially critical to the many women who must remain quiet, or "closeted," about this part of their lives in their other NGO activities. The difficulty of being "out" about one's relation or identity was a frequent topic in ongoing conversations. The risk some women felt about being identified as lesbian to their communities presented a few logistical problems—for example, how to handle the steady stream of photographers coming to shoot the lesbians in the tent. Visibility can be costly: Filipina activists at Beijing reported that two women had recently been fired from their jobs at a humanitarian NGO in Manila when their relationship became known there.

Beyond its use as a gathering site, the tent served as a key symbol, a concrete manifestation of the lesbian presence and acceptance and was, therefore, a presence organizers wanted noted in the media and representations about the conference. The lesbian tent hosted a continuous flow of visitors, including fascinated onlookers and reporters eager to file a sensationalist story. Anjana, the Thai organizer, prepared a "lesbianism for the curious" meeting where attendees were able to ask questions about this thing called lesbianism. African lesbians and bisexuals met for the first time. For the most part, the neighboring tents, passersby, and the larger NGO community received the lesbian presence with warmth and welcome. These exchanges at the lesbian tent or the "curious" workshops were important ways to demonstrate that lesbians come from all regions, classes, and ages; to show that they can be happy, well adjusted, and have children; and to convey that the problems we face come from society or the state, not from our sexuality itself.

One of the main aims of lesbian visibility at the Fourth World Conference on Women was to speak out about the particular kinds of risks, difficulties, and violations lesbians face because of their sexuality. Workshops addressed lesbian organizing around the world, specifically in "the south or difficult places" (including eastern Europe) where being visible or obtaining facilities for meeting or even printing a newsletter is extremely difficult. At workshops on lesbians in Asia, some women talked about how families coerce lesbian as well as non-lesbian women into heterosexual relations they do not want. Homophobia was in the current international news, too: the lesbians from Africa arrived at Beijing just after the president of Zimbabwe had publicly equated homosexuals with dogs, while in the United States homosexuality erupted as a hot topic in the presidential campaigns.

Outside of the explicit lesbian-themed workshops, lesbians were prominent in the larger NGO Forum as well. In a plenary session about rising conservatism, Rebeca Sevilla of Peru spoke on the specific dangers for lesbians and gays posed by fundamentalism. Daphne Scholinski, an artist from the United States, added her testimony to those of the twenty-one women from around the world at the tribunal about the violations of women's human rights. Scholinski told of her ordeal when, from the ages of fourteen to eighteen, she was incarcerated in U.S. mental institutions mainly for being a tomboy or gay.

Compiling examples of the problems faced by women who deviate from sexual and gender codes is an important part of the lesbian organizing effort. At Beijing, IGLHRC released a document that will help this organizing, called *Unspoken Rules: Sexual Orientation and Women's Human Rights,* which contains in-depth reports on the situation of lesbians in thirty-one countries.[1] Lesbians and supporters at Beijing made the case that the problems faced by women because of their sexuality are a political issue—that is, that "lesbian rights are human rights." This phrase provided the slogan for the colorful lesbian march through the NGO Forum site, which was the second largest of such protests and was lined with spectators.

The official governmental meetings at Beijing offered perhaps the most dramatic moments of lesbian visibility, especially in contrast to the earlier UN conferences. At the preparatory meetings, activists for sexual rights (guided by friends in high places) had been rapidly learning and improvising tactics to ensure that violations of women's basic rights based on sexuality were addressed by this official forum. The drafts for the official document held five paragraphs with the terms *sexual orientation, sexual rights,* or *sexual autonomy* marked for debate by brackets. In Beijing, in a bordello-like room above a disco, the "lesbian caucus" met daily to plan lobbying to include these phrases. Inspired by the direct-action method of politics, lesbians staged a peaceful protest within the UN meeting itself, displaying a banner and placards. (Two Canadian women were "arrested," prompting Bella Abzug to pose as their lawyer, but they were released without charge.)

Sexual orientation or lesbian issues emerged within a larger program that included the issues of single women, women forced into marriage, the variation of family forms—most broadly, as a woman's right to "sexual autonomy" or "sexual rights": the right to choose her sexual and intimate relations free from violence, economic risk, or political sanctions. The most successful grounds on which to argue for lesbian rights were antidiscrimination terms, since government delegates could agree that discrimination against lesbians was wrong while not agreeing to rights concerning sexuality. In the end, the term *sexual orientation* was not included in the Platform for Action. However, paragraph 96 addresses women's right to make sexual decisions free of coercion, discrimination, and violence and presents a starting point for future organizing around the UN.

By and large, the organizing strategy emphasized more the ways that sexuality involved human rights than it did development or economic concerns. But while the lobbying efforts concentrated on discrimination on the basis of sexual orientation, it is important to stress that the organizers for sexual rights at the UN and NGO meetings did not separate these issues from questions of structural adjustment, economic inequality, or political domination. Lobbyists for sexual rights also collaborated with the health and human rights caucuses and supported the Caribbean's effort to include the phrases acknowledging a "diversity of family structures" against the Vatican's formulation identifying only one legitimate family form.

In the end, the clarity of the resistance to acknowledging sexual orientation in a women's forum served lesbians well. The explicit objections presented in meetings, conversations, and official documents made it clear that sexuality is a significant issue and also showed lesbian supporters the venom of the opposition. In the one-hour debate over the term se*xual orientation*, each country was compelled to take note of an otherwise invisible issue.

Obviously, there were opponents of "sexual rights" and the lesbian presence at the Beijing conference. However, the support for lesbian issues appeared to outweigh the proponents of what are referred to as "family" or "traditional" values. Back in the preparatory meetings in New York City in March 1995, lesbians and Tibetans allied over concerns about access to the conference, an alliance that lasted through the Beijing conference. More than two hundred diverse organizations signed an IGLHRC petition for recognition of sexual rights. Furthermore, more than thirty countries expressed support for the recognition of sexual orientation or sexual rights.

The high visibility of the lesbian tent in the NGO Forum and the respectful alliances formed in the UN debates demonstrate that sexual issues and lesbian concerns now have a place within the global women's rights movement for "equality, development, peace." Speaking to the floor of the UN meeting in Beijing, Palesa Beverley Ditsie of South Africa explained the heart of the issue: "No woman can determine the direction of her own life without the ability to determine her sexuality."

NOTES

I would like to thank Rachel Rosenbloom of IGLHRC and Kate Wilson, a coordinator of the lesbian tent, for helping with this report. My participation at the Fourth World Conference on Women was made possible by grants from the Center for Lesbian and Gay Studies and Dyke TV.

1. For information on the anthology, contact IGLHRC, 1360 Mission Street, Suite 200, San Francisco, CA 94103, U.S.A.; telephone 415-255-8680, fax 415-255-8662, E-mail IGLHRC@igc.apc.org.

QUESTIONS

1. Wilson asserts that "it was *visibility* that was precisely what the lesbian organizers were after." What were some of the ways that lesbian activists achieved this visibility? Why was/is visibility so important? What are some of the problems visibility introduces?

2. According to Wilson, the second goal (after visibility) was to show that lesbian rights (and by extension, sexual rights) are human rights. What does this mean? What support for lesbian rights was demonstrated at the conference?

3. How, according to the author, can lesbian issues be seen as part of global feminism? Why is the ability to determine sexuality an important aspect of women's self-determination overall? How do sexual rights relate to other efforts concerning families or economics?

Women, Representation and Culture

Judith Mayne

How do feminists approach women and representation? The term "representation" is necessarily broad, encompassing the word (spoken and written, fact and fiction) as well as the image (still images, as in photography or painting; moving images, as in television and cinema); "high" art and popular culture. Representation encompasses newspaper articles as well as poems; family photograph albums as well as painting in museums; television sitcoms as well as experimental films. Central to all of these different kinds of representation is their constructed quality. Representations are just that, re-presentations, recreations and interpretations of the world of objects, dreams, and experiences. They require a producer, sometimes this is a single person, and sometimes a collaborative team. Representations require a medium, a form of expression—from the voice to the pen and paper (or computer keyboard and screen), from the camera to the paintbrush and canvas.

The disadvantage of a broad term like "representation" is that it covers so much, but the advantage of this wide coverage is that we can see connections between very different forms. Feminist critics in the 1970s discovered that some representations of women spanned centuries and were visible in different art forms. For instance, a common representation of women involved the madonna versus the whore. Whereas male characters would be offered an entire range of possibilities, women tended to be divided into two opposing categories, one representing impossible perfection, the other equally impossible evil, and usually it was sexuality that made the difference (women who displayed it were evil; those who didn't were good). The opposition was present in painting, in cartoons, in books, and in movies.

Usually the whore is punished and the madonna triumphs; think of the film *Fatal Attraction* (1987), for example, in which sex-crazed Alex (Glenn Close) is contrasted in virtually every imaginable way with the ideal wife and mother Beth (Anne Archer), until finally Alex is annihilated (by Beth no less). Obvious as though the opposition may be in *Fatal Attraction*, it also plays with stereotypes, for often the madonna is blonde and the whore brunette; here, just the opposite is true. Indeed, as the blonde/brunette distinction suggests, the madonna/whore distinction relies on race as well as gender, either by identifying African American womanhood exclusively in relationship to sexuality (the Jezebel stereotype), or by creating exaggerated oppositions between African American women (think of Hattie McDaniel and Butterfly McQueen in *Gone with the Wind* [1939]). Social class plays a role as well, for often the "madonna" is middle- or upper-class and the "whore" either poor or working-class (for example, the novel and various film versions of *Stella Dallas* oppose poor, trashy Stella to the upper-class woman who will eventually replace her as mother to Stella's daughter). And so too are representations of lesbianism often marked by the madonna/whore opposition; in pulp novels of the 1950s, for example, the lesbian was often characterized as sexually insatiable, a seductive menace to the heterosexual woman she attempts to seduce.

By focusing on these representations within a specific time period, for example, we can understand how certain assumptions about gender are represented in similar ways in very different forms. By examining such representations over time, within the context of a single medium, we can understand how different forms respond both to history and cultural change in a variety of ways. By looking at how gender intersects with race and class, we can understand how representation draws on the connections between different forms of social experience.

Representations rely on various forms of cultural understanding. Artists, writers and producers are a part of the very culture that they represent in their works. At the same time, some forms of representation manage to reach across time and across cultures, and to speak to different audiences in different ways. All audiences reinvent works of the past to respond to their own understandings of the world and their own needs. Feminists are no exception. In the novels of nineteenth-century British author Jane Austen, many feminists have seen explorations of women's relationships to the institutions of marriage and property that seem resoundingly contemporary, not to mention a narrative voice that observes the world with great beauty and wit.

The generation of feminist critics and researchers who began to explore and question representations in the 1960s and 1970s were guided by a number of assumptions. They shared the assumption that representations both reflect the culture from which they emerge, and have the ability to shape that culture in turn. Representation, then, is both reflective and transformative. Generations of female film viewers discovered that the movies had provided them with lessons in how to become an acceptable woman, complete with lessons in how to dress and how to catch a man. At the same time, the movies had also provided powerful fantasies of what women could be and could do, beyond looking pretty and living happily ever after with the right man. Passionate readers remembered how the world of books transported them to lands where often women were expected to act as men's inferiors, but where women also performed acts of great courage and tried to create lives that were full and meaningful. Memories of popular songs from the past were bittersweet, for when women sang they often sang of heartbreak, but just as often their voices gave hope, pleasure, and a sense of solidarity with other women.

Representation can function both to reinforce oppressive standards of feminine behavior and to imagine possibilities not typically available to women. Representation, then, is both a form of socialization and a form of utopia, representation can contribute to enforcing patriarchal stereotypes, but it can also envisage other possibilities, other ways of being. Sometimes this re-imagining involves age-old stereotypes, such as Toni Morrison's rewriting of the madonna/whore stereotypes in her 1972 novel *Sula*. Some feminist critics have tried to divide art forms between those that enforce socialization versus those that promise utopian possibilities. In feminist film studies, for example, some feminists see Hollywood cinema as inevitably corrupt insofar as images of women are concerned, and have argued that only in reinventing the cinema, in form as well as content, will it be possible to create a truly new, feminist cinema. From this vantage point, a film like *Thelma and Louise* (1991) ultimately reinforces the impossibility of women's autonomy, and only in independent films like Cheryl Dunye's *Watermelon Woman* (1996) do we see a truly promising revision of women's lives. Others have seen Hollywood cinema as less monolithic, and have argued that depending on the kind of film and the way it is made, it is possible to see Hollywood films as speaking to women in powerful and not always simply oppressive ways. From this vantage point, *Thelma and Louise* is important for Callie Khouri's screenplay, for Geena Davis's and Susan Sarandon's performances, and for a tale of female friendship that revises many assumptions of a type of film—the buddy film—usually reserved for men.

In the early 1970s, it was common to assume that works by male artists or producers would be more likely to reflect patriarchal assumptions than those by women. That assumption led to various attempts to rediscover female writers, artists and producers whose works had not been remembered. At the same time, this search for notable women in the past led feminists to reconsider just what constitutes "art" in the first place. To be sure, some great women artists and writers had been obscured from official histories. But other women had produced works of great beauty—quilts, diaries, songs—that were not even considered art. The broad term "representation" thus encourages us to see all images, stories, and texts as potentially interesting.

FURTHER READINGS

Deepwell, Katy, ed. *New feminist art criticism: critical strategies*. Manchester University Press; New York: St. Martin's Press, c 1995.

Haskell, Molly. *From Reverence to Rape*. New York: Holt, Rinehart and Winston, 1974.

Kuhn, Annette. *The Power of the Image: Essays on Representation and Sexuality*. London and Boston: Rutledge & Kegan Paul, 1985.

Showalter, Elaine, ed. *The New Feminist Criticism: Essays on Women, Literature, and Theory*. New York: Pantheon, 1985.

Skeggs, Beverley, ed. *Feminist Cultural Theory: Process and Production.* Manchester University Press, New York: St. Martin's Press, 1995.

Walker, Alice. *In Search of Our Mothers' Gardens: Womanist Prose.* San Diego: Harcourt Brace Jovanovich, 1983.

Dash, Julie. *Daughters of the Dust: The Making of an African-American Woman's Film.* Key Note International Distribution Co., 1992.

Douglas, Susan J. *Where the Girls Are: Growing Up Female with the Mass Media.* New York: Random House, 1994.

Hooks, Bell. *Black Looks: Race and Representation.* Boston, MA: South End P, 1992.

Kim, Elaine H, Lilia V. Villanueva and Asian Women United. *Making More Waves: New Writing by Asian American Women.* Beacon P, 1997.

Lee, Valerie. *Granny Midwives and Black Women Writers: Double-Dutched Readings.* New York: Routledge, 1996.

Patridge, Elizabeth. *Dorothea Lange: A Visual Life.* Smithsonian Institute P, 1994.

Robolledo, Tey Diana and Elena S. Rivero, Eds. *Infinite Divisions: An Anthology of Chicana Literature.* Univ. of Arizona P, 1993.

Sontag, Susan. *On Photography.* Anchor P, 1990.

THE BODY POLITIC
(1995)

Abra Fortune Chernik

Body hatred is something many women share in what Abra Chernik terms a "diet culture," but the life-threatening aspects of anorexia and bulimia are sometimes dismissed. In the following narrative from Listen Up! Voices From the Next Feminist Generation, *screenwriter and activist Abra Chernik describes her hospitalization for anorexia and her struggle to overcome the illusion of power and control that she felt in her anorexic world.*

My body possesses solidness and curve, like the ocean. My weight mingles with Earth's pull, drawing me onto the sand. I have not always sent waves into the world. I flew off once, for five years, and swirled madly like a cracking brown leaf in the salty autumn wind. I wafted, dried out, apathetic.

I had no weight in the world during my years of anorexia. Curled up inside my thinness, a refugee in a cocoon of hunger, I lost the capacity to care about myself or others. I starved my body and twitched in place as those around me danced in the energy of shared existence and progressed in their lives. When I graduated from college crowned with academic honors, professors praised my potential. I wanted only to vanish.

It took three months of hospitalization and two years of out-patient psychotherapy for me to learn to nourish myself and to live in a body that expresses strength and honesty in its shape. I accepted my right and my obligation to take up room with my figure, voice and spirit. I remembered how to tumble forward and touch the world that holds me. I chose the ocean as my guide.

Who disputes the ocean's fullness?

Growing up in New York City, I did not care about the feminist movement. Although I attended an all-girls high school, we read mostly male authors and studied the history of men. Embracing mainstream culture without question, I learned about womanhood from fashion magazines, Madison Avenue and Hollywood. I dismissed feminist alternatives as foreign and offensive, swathed as they were in stereotypes that threatened my adolescent need for conformity.

Puberty hit late; I did not complain. I enjoyed living in the lanky body of a tall child and insisted on the title of "girl." If anyone referred to me as a "young woman," I would cry out, horrified, "Do not call me the W word!" But at sixteen years old, I could no longer deny my fate. My stomach and breasts rounded. Curly black hair sprouted in the most embarrassing places. Hips swelled from a once-flat plane. Interpreting maturation as an unacceptable lapse into fleshiness, I resolved to eradicate the physical symptoms of my impending womanhood.

Magazine articles, television commercials, lunchroom conversation, gymnastics coaches and write-ups on models had saturated me with diet savvy. Once I decided to lose weight, I quickly turned expert. I dropped hot chocolate from my regular breakfast order at the Skyline Diner. I replaced lunches of peanut butter and Marshmallow Fluff sandwiches with small platters of cottage cheese and cantaloupe. I eliminated dinner altogether and blunted my appetite with Tab, Camel Lights, and Carefree bubble gum. When furious craving overwhelmed my resolve and I swallowed an extra something, I would flee to the nearest bathroom to purge my mistake.

Within three months, I had returned my body to its preadolescent proportions and had manipulated my monthly period into drying up. Over the next five years, I devoted my life to losing my weight. I came to resent the body in which I lived, the body that threatened to develop, the body whose hunger I despised but could not extinguish. If I neglected a workout or added a pound or ate a bite too many, I would stare in the mirror and drown myself in a tidal wave of criticism. Hatred of my body generalized to hatred of myself as a person, and self-referential labels such as "pig," "failure" and "glutton" allowed me to believe that I deserved punishment. My self-hatred became fuel for the self-mutilating behaviors of the eating disorder.

As my body shrank, so did my world. I starved away my power and vision, my energy and inclinations. Obsessed with dieting, I allowed relationships, passions and identity to wither. I pulled back from the world, off of the beach, out of the sand. The waves of my existence ceased to roll beyond the inside of my skin.

And society applauded my shrinking. Pound after pound the applause continued, like the pounding ocean outside the door of my beach house.

The word "anorexia" literally means "loss of appetite." But as an anorexic, I felt hunger thrashing inside my body. I denied my appetite, ignored it, but never lost it. Sometimes the pangs twisted so sharply, I feared they would consume the meat of my heart. On desperate nights I rose in a flannel nightgown and allowed myself to eat an unplanned something.

No matter how much I ate, I could not soothe the pangs. Standing in the kitchen at midnight, spotlighted by the blue-white light of the open refrigerator, I would frantically feed my neglected appetite: the Chinese food I had not touched at dinner; ice cream and whipped cream; microwaved bread; cereal and chocolate milk; doughnuts and bananas. Then, solid sadness inside my gut, swelling agitation, a too-big meal I would not digest. In the bathroom I would rip off my shirt, tie up my hair, and prepare to execute the desperate ritual, again. I would ram the back of my throat with a toothbrush handle, crying, impatient, until the food rushed up. I would vomit until the toilet filled and I emptied, until I forgave myself, until I felt ready to try my life again. Standing up from my position over the toilet, wiping my mouth, I would believe that I was safe. Looking in the mirror through puffy eyes in a tumescent face, I would promise to take care of myself. Kept awake by the fast, confused beating of my heart and the ache in my chest, I would swear I did not miss the world outside. Lost within myself, I almost died.

By the time I entered the hospital, a mess of protruding bones defined my body, and the bones of my emaciated life rattled me crazy. I carried a pillow around because it hurt to sit down, and I shivered with cold in sultry July. Clumps of brittle hair clogged the drain when I showered, and blackened eyes appeared to sink into my head. My vision of reality wrinkled and my disposition turned mercurial as I slipped into starvation psychosis, a condition associated with severe malnutrition. People told me that I resembled a concentration camp prisoner, a chemotherapy patient, a famine victim or a fashion model.

In the hospital, I examined my eating disorder under the lenses of various therapies. I dissected my childhood, my family structure, my intimate relationships, my belief systems. I participated in experiential therapies of movement, art and psychodrama. I learned to use words instead of eating patterns to communicate my feelings. And still I refused to gain more than a minimal amount of weight.

I felt powerful as an anorexic. Controlling my body yielded an illusion of control over my life; I received incessant praise for my figure despite my sickly mien, and my frailty manipulated family and friends into protecting me from conflict. I had reduced my world to a plate of steamed carrots, and over this tiny kingdom I proudly crowned myself queen.

I sat cross-legged on my hospital bed for nearly two months before I earned an afternoon pass to go to the mall with my mother. The privilege came just in time; I felt unbearably large and desperately wanted a new outfit under which to hide gained weight. At the mall, I searched for two hours before finally discovering, in the maternity section at Macy's, a shirt large enough to cover what I perceived as my enormous body.

With an hour left on my pass, I spotted a sign on a shop window: "Body Fat Testing, $3.00." I suggested to my mother that we split up for ten minutes; she headed to Barnes & Noble, and I snuck into the fitness store.

I sat down in front of a machine hooked up to a computer, and a burly young body builder fired questions at me:

"Age?"

"Twenty-one."

"Height?"

"Five nine."

"Weight?"

"Ninety-nine."

The young man punched my statistics into his keyboard and pinched my arm with clippers wired to the testing machine. In a moment, the computer spit out my results. "Only ten percent body fat! Unbelievably healthy. The average for a woman your age is twenty-five percent. Fantastic! You're this week's blue ribbon winner."

I stared at him in disbelief. *Winner? Healthy? Fantastic?* I glanced around at the other customers in the store, some of whom had congregated to watch my testing, and I felt embarrassed by his praise. And then I felt furious. Furious at this man and at the society that programmed him for their ignorant approbation of my illness and my suffering.

"I am dying of anorexia," I whispered. "Don't congratulate me."

I spent my remaining month in the hospital supplementing psychotherapy with an independent examination of eating disorders from a social and political point of view. I needed to understand why society would reward my starvation and encourage my vanishing. In the bathroom, a mirror on the open door behind me reflected my backside in a mirror over the sink. Vertebrae poked at my skin, ribs hung like wings over chiseled hip bones, the two sides of my buttocks did not touch. I had not seen this view of myself before.

In writing, I recorded instances in which my eating disorder had tangled the progress of my life and thwarted my relationships. I filled three and a half Mead marble notebooks. Five years' worth of: *I wouldn't sit with Daddy when he was alone in the hospital because I needed to go jogging; I told Derek not to visit me because I couldn't throw up when he was there; I almost failed my comprehensive exams because I was so hungry; I spent my year at Oxford with my head in the toilet bowl; I wouldn't eat the dinner my friends cooked me for my nineteenth birthday because I knew they had used oil in the recipe; I told my family not to come to my college graduation because I didn't want to miss a day at the gym or have to eat a restaurant meal.* And on and on for hundreds of pages.

This honest account of my life dissolved the illusion of

anorexic power. I saw myself naked in the truth of my pain, my loneliness, my obsessions, my craziness, my selfishness, my defeat. I also recognized the social and political implications of consuming myself with the trivialities of calories and weight. At college, I had watched as classmates involved themselves in extracurricular clubs, volunteer work, politics and applications for jobs and graduate schools. Obsessed with exercising and exhausted by starvation, I did not even consider joining in such pursuits. Despite my love of writing and painting and literature, despite ranking at the top of my class, I wanted only to teach aerobics. Despite my adolescent days as a loud-mouthed, rambunctious class leader, I had grown into a silent, hungry young woman.

And society preferred me this way: hungry, fragile, crazy. *Winner! Healthy! Fantastic!* I began reading feminist literature to further understand the disempowerment of women in our culture. I digested the connection between a nation of starving, self-obsessed women and the continued success of the patriarchy. I also cultivated an awareness of alternative models of womanhood. In the stillness of the hospital library, new voices in my life rose from printed pages to echo my rage and provide the conception of my feminist consciousness.

I had been willing to accept self-sabotage, but now I refused to sacrifice myself to a society that profited from my pain. I finally understood that my eating disorder symbolized more than "personal psychodynamic trauma." Gazing in the mirror at my emaciated body, I observed a woman held up by her culture as the physical ideal because she was starving, self-obsessed and powerless, a woman called beautiful because she threatened no one except herself. Despite my intelligence, my education, and my supposed Manhattan sophistication, I had believed all the lies; I had almost given my life in order to achieve the sickly impotence that this culture aggressively links with female happiness, love and success. And everything I had to offer to the world, every tumbling wave, every thought and every passion, nearly died inside me.

As long as society resists female power, fashion will call healthy women physically flawed. As long as society accepts the physical, sexual and economic abuse of women, popular culture will prefer women who resemble little girls. Sitting in the hospital the summer after my college graduation, I grasped the absurdity of a nation of adult women dying to grow small.

Armed with this insight, I loosened the grip of the starvation disease on my body. I determined to recreate myself based on an image of a woman warrior. I remembered my ocean, and I took my first bite.

Gaining weight and getting my head out of the toilet bowl was the most political act I have ever committed.

I left the hospital and returned home to Fire Island. Living at the shore in those wintry days of my new life, I wrapped myself in feminism as I hunted sea shells and role models. I wanted to feel proud of my womanhood. I longed to accept and honor my body's fullness.

During the process of my healing, I had hoped that I would be able to skip the memory of anorexia like a cold pebble into the dark winter sea. I had dreamed that in relinquishing my obsessive chase after a smaller body, I would be able to come home to rejoin those whom I had left in order to starve, rejoin them to live together as healthy, powerful women. But as my body has grown full, I have sensed a hollowness in the lives of women all around me that I had not noticed when I myself stood hollow. I have made it home only to find myself alone.

Out in the world again, I hear the furious thumping dance of body hatred echoing every place I go. Friends who once appeared wonderfully carefree in ordering late-night french fries turn out not to eat breakfast or lunch. Smart, talented, creative women talk about dieting and overeating and hating the beach because they look terrible in bathing suits. Famous women give interviews insulting their bodies and bragging about bicycling twenty-four miles the day they gave birth.

I had looked forward to rejoining society after my years of anorexic exile. Ironically, in order to preserve my health, my recovery has included the development of a consciousness that actively challenges the images and ideas that define this culture. Walking down Madison Avenue and passing emaciated women, I say to myself, *those women are sick*. When smacked with a diet commercial, I remind myself, *I don't do that anymore*. I decline invitations to movies that feature anorexic actors, I will not participate in discussions about dieting, and I refuse to shop in stores that cater to women with eating-disordered figures.

Though I am critical of diet culture, I find it nearly impossible to escape. Eating disorders have woven their way into the fabric of my society. On television, in print, on food packaging, in casual conversation and in windows of clothing stores populated by ridiculously gaunt mannequins, messages to lose my weight and control my appetite challenge my recovered fullness. Finally at home in my body, I recognize myself as an island in a sea of eating disorders, a sea populated predominantly by young women.

A perversion of nature by society has resulted in a phenomenon whereby women feel safer when starving than when eating. Losing our weight boosts self-esteem, while nourishing our bodies evokes feelings of self-doubt and self-loathing.

When our bodies take up more space than a size eight (as most of our bodies do), we say, *too big*. When our appetites demand more than a Lean Cuisine, we say, *too much*. When we want a piece of a friend's birthday cake, we say, *too bad*. Don't eat too much, don't talk too loudly, don't take up too much space, don't take from the world. Be pleasant or crazy, but don't seem hungry. Remember, a new study shows that men prefer women who eat salad for dinner over women who eat burgers and fries.

So we keep on shrinking, starving away our wildness, our power, our truth.

Hiding our curves under long T-shirts at the beach, sitting silently and fidgeting while others eat dessert, sneaking back into the kitchen late at night to binge and hating ourselves the next day, skipping breakfast, existing on diet soda and cigarettes, adding up calories and subtracting everything else. We accept what is horribly wrong in our lives and fight what is beautiful and right.

Over the past three years, feminism has taught me to honor the fullness of my womanhood and the solidness of the body that hosts my life. In feminist circles I have found mentors, strong women who live with power, passion and purpose. And yet, even in groups of feminists, my love and acceptance of my body remains unusual.

Eating disorders affect us all on both a personal and a political level. The majority of my peers—including my feminist peers—still measure their beauty against anorexic ideals. Even among feminists, body hatred and chronic dieting continue to consume lives. Friends of anorexics beg them to please start eating; then these friends go home and continue their own diets. Who can deny that the millions of young women caught in the net of disordered eating will frustrate the potential of the next wave of feminism?

Sometimes my empathy dissolves into frustration and rage at our situation. For the first time in history, young women have the opportunity to create a world in our image. But many of us concentrate instead on recreating the shape of our thighs.

As young feminists, we must place unconditional acceptance of our bodies at the top of our political agenda. We must claim our bodies as our own to love and honor in their infinite shapes and sizes. Fat, thin, soft, hard, puckered, smooth, our bodies are our homes. By nourishing our bodies, we care for and love ourselves on the most basic level. When we deny ourselves physical food, we go hungry emotionally, psychologically, spiritually and politically. We must challenge ourselves to eat and digest, and allow society to call us too big. We will understand their message to mean too powerful.

Time goes by quickly. One day we will blink and open our eyes as old women. If we spend all our energy keeping our bodies small, what will we have to show for our lives when we reach the end? I hope we have more than a group of fashionably skinny figures.

QUESTIONS

1. How can individual eating problems actually be considered political problems? What factors contribute to the existence of eating problems?

2. What is the meaning and significance of "body hatred"? What are the effects of body hatred for both the individual and society?

3. How does Chernik change through the course of her narrative? What issues does Chernik face in her struggle for personal growth as a woman? How does she feel about her experiences?

HOMAGE TO MY HIPS,
HOMAGE TO MY HAIR
(1980)

Lucille Clifton

In each of the following two poems, Lucille Clifton challenges Euro-American traditional standards of beauty, celebrating that which is culturally defined as falling outside of beauty norms—big hips and nappy hair. Clifton is the author of several poetry books including good woman: poems *and a memoir 1969–1980, as well as a number of children's books. She currently lives in Maryland and California, and she teaches at the University of Santa Cruz.*

Homage to My Hips
these hips are big hips
they need space to
move around in.
they don't fit into little
petty places. these hips
are free hips.

they don't like to be held back.
these hips have never been enslaved,
they go where they want to go
they do what they want to do.
these hips are mighty hips.
these hips are magic hips.
I have known them
to put a spell on a man and
spin him like a top!

Homage to My Hair

when i feel her jump up and dance
i hear the music! my God
i'm talking about my nappy hair!
she is a challenge to your hand
black man,
she is as tasty on your tongue as good greens
black man,
she can touch your mind
with her electric fingers and
the grayer she do get, good God,
the blacker she do be!

QUESTIONS

1. What do the poems indicate about specific problems Black women face in their confrontation with beauty norms?

2. In what ways are U.S. beauty norms racist? Think of some examples of how this racism is reflected in our culture.

3. Why do you think Clifton celebrates her hips and hair in these poems?

WHY THE SHIRELLES MATTERED (1994)

Susan Douglas

According to Susan Douglas, professor of media studies at Hampshire College and author of Where the Girls Are: Growing Up Female with the Mass Media, *pop music, particularly "girl group" music of the early 1960s, became the one area of popular culture in which adolescent female voices could be heard. The music, the lyrics, and its performances reflected teenage confusion and ambivalence about love, sexual desire, and conventional gender norms. Douglas views "girl groups" like the Shirelles, the Shangri-Las, and the Supremes as icons of popular teen culture.*

OK—here's a test. Get a bunch of women in their thirties and forties and put them in a room with a stereo. Turn up the volume to the "incurs temporary deafness" level and play "Will You Love Me Tomorrow" and see how many know the words—all the words—by heart. If the answer is 100 percent, these are bona fide American baby boomers. Any less, and the group has been infil-

trated by impostors, pod people, Venusians. But even more interesting is the fact that non-baby boomers, women both older and
younger than my generation, adore this music too, and cling to the
lyrics like a life raft.

Why is it that, over thirty years after this song was number
one in the country, it still evokes in us such passion, such longing,
such euphoria, and such an irresistible desire to sing very loudly
off key and not care who hears us? And it's not just this song, it's
girl group music in general, from "He's So Fine" to "Nowhere to
Run" to "Sweet Talkin' Guy." Today, the "oldies" station is one of
the most successful FM formats going, in no small part because
when these songs come on the radio, baby boomers get that
faraway, knowing, contented look on their faces that prompts
them to scream along with the lyrics while running red lights on
the way home from work. None of this is silly—there's a good
reason why, even on our deathbeds, we'll still know the words to
"Leader of the Pack."

First of all, girl group music was really about us—girls. When
rock 'n' roll swiveled onto the national scene in the mid-1950s and
united a generation in opposition to their parents, it was music
performed by rebellious and sexually provocative young men.
Elvis Presley was, of course, rock 'n' roll's most famous and
insistently masculine star—in 1956, five of the nine top singles of
the year were by Elvis. At the same time, there would be weeks,
even months, when no woman or female group had a hit among
the top fifteen records. When women in the fifties did have hits,
they were about the moon, weddings, some harmless dreamboat,
like Annette's "Tall Paul," or maybe about kissing. But they were
never, ever about doing the wild thing.

Then, in December 1960, the Shirelles hit number one with
"Will You Love Me Tomorrow"; it was the first time a girl group,
and one composed of four black teenagers, had cracked the number one slot. And these girls were not singing about doggies in
windows or old Cape Cod. No, the subject matter here was a little
different. They were singing about whether or not to go all the
way and wondering whether the boyfriend, so seemingly full of
heartfelt, earnest love in the night, would prove to be an opportu-
nistic, manipulative, lying cad after he got his way, or whether he
would, indeed, still be filled with love in the morning. Should the
girl believe everything she'd heard about going all the way and
boys losing respect for girls who did? Or should she believe the

boy in her arms who was hugging and kissing her (and doing who knows what else) and generally making her feel real good?

Even though this song was about sex, it didn't rely on the musical instrument so frequently used to connote sex in male rockers' songs, the saxophone. Saxes were banished, as were electric guitars; instead, an entire string section of an orchestra provided the counterpoint to Shirley Owens's haunting, earthy, and provocative lead vocals. The producer, Luther Dixon, who had previously worked with Perry Como and Pat Boone, even overlaid the drumbeats with violins, so it sounded as if the strings gave the song its insistent, pulsing rhythm. While Owens's alto voice vibrated with teen girl angst and desire, grounding the song in fleshly reality, violin arpeggios fluttered through like birds, and it was on their wings that our erotic desires took flight and gained a more acceptable spiritual dimension. It was this brilliant juxtaposition of the sentimentality of the violins and the sensuality of the voice that made the song so perfect, because it was simultaneously lush and spare, conformist and daring, euphemistic yet dead-on honest. The tens of millions of girls singing along could be starry-eyed and innocent, but they could also be sophisticated and knowing. They could be safe and sing about love, or dangerous and sing about sex. "Will You Love Me Tomorrow" was about a traditional female topic, love, but it was also about female longing and desire, including sexual desire. And, most important, it was about having a choice. For these girls, the decision to have sex was now a choice, and *this* was new. This was, in fact, revolutionary. Girl group music gave expression to our struggles with the possibilities and dangers of the Sexual Revolution.

What were you to do if you were a teenage girl in the early and mid-1960s, your hormones catapulting you between desire and paranoia, elation and despair, horniness and terror? You didn't know which instincts to act on and which ones to suppress. You also weren't sure whom to listen to since, by the age of fourteen, you'd decided that neither your mother nor your father knew anything except how to say no and perhaps the lyrics to a few Andy Williams songs. For answers—real answers—many of us turned to the record players, radios, and jukeboxes of America. And what we heard were the voices of teenage girls singing about—and dignifying—our most basic concern: how to act around boys when so much seemed up for grabs. What were you to do to survive all those raging hormones? Why, dance, of course.

There's been a lot of talk, academic analysis, and the like about how Elvis Presley and rock 'n' roll made rebelliousness acceptable for boys. But what about the girls? Did girl group music help *us* become rebels? Before you say "no way" and cite "I Will Follow Him," "Chapel of Love," and "I Wanna Be Bobby's Girl" to substantiate your point, hear me out. Girl group music has been denied its rightful place in history by a host of male music critics who've either ignored it or trashed it. Typical is this pronouncement, by one of the contributors to *The Rolling Stone History of Rock & Roll*: "The female group of the early 1960s served to drive the concept of art completely away from rock 'n' roll. . . . I feel this genre represents the low point in the history of rock 'n' roll." Nothing could be more wrongheaded, or more ignorant of the role this music played in girls' lives. It would be ideal if this section of the book were accompanied by a customized CD replaying all these fabulous songs for you. Since that's not possible, I do urge you to listen to this music again, and to hear all the warring impulses, desires, and voices it contained.

By the late 1950s, Tin Pan Alley realized that Perry Como, Doris Day, and Mantovani and his orchestra weren't cutting it with the fastest-growing market segment in America, teenagers. Even Pat Boone was hopelessly square, having foisted on us the insufferable "April Love" and his goody-two-shoes advice book to teens, *'Twixt Twelve and Twenty*, which said kissing "for fun" was dangerous. Music publishers and producers grasped two key trends: rock 'n' roll was here to stay, and there was this flourishing market out there, not just boys, but girls, millions of them, ready and eager to buy. And they were not buying the Lennon Sisters or Patti Page. At the same time, the proliferation of transistor radios meant that this music could be taken and heard almost everywhere, becoming the background music for our desires, hopes, and fears, the background music to our individual and collective autobiographies.

Teenage songwriters like Carole King and Ellie Greenwich got jobs in the Brill Building in New York, the center of pop music production in America, and in the aftermath of the Shirelles hit, all kinds of girl groups and girl singers appeared, from the poufskirted Angels ("My Boyfriend's Back") to the cute and innocent Dixie Cups to the eat-my-dirt, in-your-face, badass Shangri-Las. There was an explosion in what has come to be called "girl talk" music, the lyrics and beat of which still occupy an inordinately large portion of the right—or is it the left?—side of my brain.

The most important thing about this music, the reason it spoke to us so powerfully, was that it gave voice to all the warring selves inside us struggling, blindly and with a crushing sense of insecurity, to forge something resembling a coherent identity. Even though the girl groups were produced and managed by men, it was in their music that the contradictory messages about female sexuality and rebelliousness were most poignantly and authentically expressed. In the early 1960s, pop music became the one area of popular culture in which adolescent female voices could be clearly heard. They sang about the pull between the need to conform and the often overwhelming desire to rebel, about the tension between restraint and freedom, and about the rewards—and costs—of prevailing gender roles. They sang, in other words, about getting mixed messages and about being ambivalent in the face of the upheaval in sex roles. That loss of self, the fusing of yourself with another, larger-than-life persona that girls felt as they sang along was at least as powerful as what they felt in a darkened movie theater. And singing along with one another, we shared common emotions and physical reactions to the music.

This music was, simultaneously, deeply personal and highly public, fusing our neurotic, quivering inner selves with the neurotic, quivering inner selves of others in an effort to find strength and confidence in numbers. We listened to this music in the darkness of our bedrooms, driving around in our parents' cars, on the beach, making out with some boy, and we danced to it—usually with other girls—in the soda shops, basements, and gymnasiums of America. This music burrowed into the everyday psychodramas of our adolescence, forever intertwined with our most private, exhilarating, and embarrassing memories. This music exerted such a powerful influence on us, one that we may barely have recognized, because of this process of identification. By superimposing our own dramas, from our own lives, onto each song, each of us could assume an active role in shaping the song's meaning. Songs that were hits around the country had very particular associations and meanings for each listener, and although they were mass-produced they were individually interpreted. The songs were ours—but they were also everyone else's. We were all alone, but we weren't really alone at all. In this music, we found solidarity as girls.

Some girl group songs, like "I Will Follow Him," allowed us to assume the familiar persona *Cinderella* had trained us for, the selfless masochist whose identity came only from being some appendage to a man. As we sang along with Dionne Warwick's "Walk on By," we were indeed abject martyrs to love, luxuriating in our own self-pity. But other songs addressed our more feisty and impatient side, the side unwilling to sit around and wait for the boy to make the first move. In "tell him" songs like "Easier Said Than Done," "Wishin' and Hopin'," and, of course, "Tell Him," girls were advised to abandon the time-wasting and possibly boy-losing stance of passively waiting for *him* to make the first move. We were warned that passivity might cost us our man, and we were urged to act immediately and unequivocally, before some more daring girl got there first. Girls were urged to take up a previously male prerogative—to be active agents of their own love lives and to go out and court the boy. Regardless of how girls actually be-haved—and I know from personal experience that what was deri-sively called "boy chasing" was on the rise—now there were lyrics in girls' heads that said, "Don't be passive, it will cost you."

Was being cautious too safe? Was being daring too risky? Girl group music acknowledged—even celebrated—our confusion and ambivalence. Some of us wanted to be good girls, and some of us wanted to be bad. But most of us wanted to get away with being both, and girl group music let us try on and act out a host of identities, from traditional, obedient girlfriend to brassy, indepen-dent rebel, and lots in between. We could even do this in the same song, for often the lead singer represented one point of view and the backup singers another, so the very wars raging in our own heads about how to behave, what pose to strike, were enacted in one two-minute hit single.

Few songs capture this more perfectly than one of the true girl group greats, "Sweet Talkin' Guy" by the Chiffons. Here we have a tune about a deceitful and heartless charmer who acts like he loves you one day and moves on to another girl the next. Nonethe-less, since he's "sweeter than sugar" (ooh-ooh) with "kisses like wine (oh he's so fine)," this heel is irresistible. The lead singer warns other girls to stay away from such a boy, since he'll only break their hearts, but she also confesses he is "my kinda guy." The female chorus backs her up, acknowledging that it is indeed understandable to be swept up by such a cad.

On the face of it, we have lyrics about the unrequited love of a young woman with, no doubt, a few masochistic tendencies. But the song achieves much more. With the layering of voices over and against one another, some of them alto and some of them soprano, we have a war between resisting such boys and suc-cumbing to them. The music, with its driving beat and a tambou-rine serving as metronome, is dance music. At the end of the song the layered vocal harmonies run ecstatically up the octaves, like girls running jubilantly across a field, ending with a euphoric chord that suggests, simultaneously, that young female love will win in the end and that it will transcend male brutishness. Singing along to a song like this, girls could change voice, becoming singing ventriloquists for different stances toward the same boy, the same situation. As altos, sopranos, or both, back and forth, we could love and denounce such boys, we could warn against our own victimization, yet fall prey to its sick comforts. We could feel how desire—irresistible, irrational, timeless—was shaping our destinies. The euphoric musical arrangement made us feel even more strongly that the power to love and to dream would enable us somehow to burst through the traps of history. In "Sweet Talkin' Guy," being divided against yourself is normal, natural, true: the song celebrates the fact not just that girls *do* have conflict-ing subjective stances but that, to get by, they *must*. Yes, we can't help loving them, even when they're bastards, but we have to be able to name how they hurt us, and we must share those warnings with other girls. And if we're dancing while we do it, moving our bodies autonomously, or in unison with other girls, well, maybe we'll escape after all.

Girl group songs were, by turns, boastful, rebellious, and self-abnegating, and through them girls could assume different perso-nas, some of them strong and empowering and others masochistic and defeating. As girls listened to their radios and record players, they could be martyrs to love ("Please Mr. Postman"), sexual aggressors ("Beechwood 4-5789"), fearsome Amazons protecting their men ("Don't Mess with Bill" and "Don't Say Nothin' Bad About My Baby"), devoted, selfless girlfriends ("My Guy," "I Will Follow Him"), taunting, competitive brats ("Judy's Turn to Cry," "My Boyfriend's Back"), sexual sophisticates ("It's in His Kiss"), and, occasionally, prefeminists ("Don't Make Me Over" and "You Don't Own Me"). The Shirelles themselves, in hit after hit, as-sumed different stances, from the faithful romantic ("Soldier Boy," "Dedicated to the One I Love") to knowing adviser ("Mama Said," "Foolish Little Girl") to sexual slave ("Baby, It's You"). The songs were about escaping from yet acquiescing to the demands of a male-dominated society, in which men called the shots but girls could still try to give them a run for their money. Girls in these songs enjoyed being looked at with desire, but they also enjoyed looking with desire themselves. The singers were totally confident; they were abjectly insecure. Some songs said do and others said don't. Sometimes the voice was of an assertive, no-nonsense girl out to get the guy or showing off her boyfriend to her friends. At other times, the voice was that of the passive object, yearning patiently to be discovered and loved. Often the girl tried to get into the boy's head and imagined the boy regarding her as the object of his desire. Our pathetic struggles and anxieties about popularity were glamorized and dignified in these songs.

In girl group music, girls talked to each other confidentially, primarily about boys and sex. The songs took our angst-filled conversations, put them to music, and gave them a good beat. Some songs, like "He's So Fine" (doo lang, doo lang, doo lang), picked out a cute boy from the crowd and plotted how he would be hooked. In this song the choice was clearly hers, not his. Songs also re-created images of a clot of girls standing around in their mohair sweaters assessing the male talent and, well, looking over boys the way boys had always looked over girls. Other songs, like "Playboy" or "Too Many Fish in the Sea," warned girls about two-timing Romeo types who didn't deserve the time of day, and the sassy, defiant singers advised girls to tell boys who didn't treat them right to take a hike. Opening with a direct address to their sisters—"Look here, girls, take this advice"—the Marvelettes passed on what sounded like age-old female wisdom: "My mother once told me something/And every word is true/Don't waste your time on a fella/Who doesn't love you." Urging the listener to "stand tall," the lead singer asserted, "I don't want nobody that don't want me/Ain't gonna love nobody that don't love me."

The absolute necessity of female collusion in the face of thoughtless or mystifying behavior by boys bound these songs together, and bound the listeners to the singers in a knowing sorority. They knew things about boys and love that they shared with each other, and this shared knowledge—smarter, more deeply intuitive, more worldly wise than any male locker room talk—provided a powerful bonding between girls, a kind of bonding boys didn't have. And while boys were often identified as the love object, they were also identified as the enemy. So while some of the identities we assumed as we sang along were those of the traditional, passive, obedient, lovesick girl, each of us could also be a sassy, assertive, defiant girl who intended to have more control over her life—or at least her love life. In numerous advice songs, from "Mama Said" to "You Can't Hurry Love," the message that girls knew a thing or two, and that they would share that knowledge with one another to beat the odds in a man's world, circulated confidently.

Other songs fantasized about beating a different set of odds—the seeming inevitability, for white, middle-class girls, of being married off to some boring, respectable guy with no sense of danger or adventure, someone like David Nelson or one of Fred MacMurray's three sons. Here we come to the rebel category—"Leader of the Pack," "Uptown," "He's a Rebel," "Give Him a Great Big Kiss," and "He's Sure the Boy I Love." Academic zeros, on unemployment, clad in leather jackets, sporting dirty fingernails, and blasting around on motorcycles, the boy heroes in these songs were every suburban parent's nightmare, the boys they loved to hate. By allying herself romantically and morally with the rebel hero, the girl singer and listener proclaimed her independence from society's predictable expectations about her inevitable domestication. There is a role reversal here, too—the girls are gathered in a group, sharing information about their boyfriends, virtually eyeing them up and down, while the rebel heroes simply remain the passive objects of their gaze and their talk. And the girls who sang these songs, like the Shangri-Las, dressed the part of the defiant bad girl who stuck her tongue out at parental and middle-class authority. The Ronettes, whose beehives scraped the ceiling and whose eyeliner was thicker than King Tut's, wore spiked heels and skintight dresses with slits up the side as they begged some boy to "Be My Baby." They combined fashion rebellion with in-your-face sexual insurrection.

In "Will You Love Me Tomorrow," Shirley Owens asked herself, Should she or shouldn't she? Of course, the question quickly became, Should I or shouldn't I? The answer wasn't clear, and we heard plenty of songs in which girls found themselves smack in the grip of sexual desire. Sexuality emerged as an eternal ache, a kind of irresistible, unquenchable tension. But in the early 1960s, sex and sexual desire were still scary for many girls. The way many of these songs were produced—orchestrated with violins instead of with electric guitars or saxophones—muted the sexual explicitness and made it more romantic, more spiritual, more safe. "And Then He Kissed Me" alluded to some kind of new kiss tried on the singer by her boyfriend, one she really liked and wanted to have a lot more of. In "Heat Wave," Martha Reeves sang at the top of her lungs about being swept up in a sexual fever that just wouldn't break, and the whispering, bedroom-voiced lead in "I'm Ready" confessed that she didn't really know quite what she was supposed to do but that she was sure ready to learn—right now. Claudine Clark desperately begged her mother to let her go off to the source of the "Party Lights," where one helluva party was happening, and she sounded like someone who had been in Alcatraz for twenty years and would simply explode if she didn't get out.

The contradictions of being a teenage girl in the early and mid-1960s also percolated from the conflict between the lyrics of the song and the beat of the music. Girl group music had emerged at the same time as all these new dance crazes that redefined how boys and girls did—or, more accurately, did not—dance with each other. Chubby Checker's 1960 hit "The Twist" revolution-ized teenage dancing, because it meant that boys and girls didn't have to hold hands anymore, boys didn't have to lead and girls didn't have to follow, so girls had a lot more autonomy and control as they danced. Plus, dancing was one of the things girls usually did much better than boys. As the twist gave way to the locomotion, the Bristol stomp, the mashed potato, the pony, the monkey, the slop, the jerk, and the frug, the dances urged us to loosen up our chests and our butts, and learn how to shimmy, grind, and thrust. This was something my friends and I did with gleeful abandon.

Many of us felt most free and exhilarated while we were dancing, so bouncing around to a song like "Chains" or "No-where to Run" put us smack-dab between feelings of liberation and enslavement, between a faith in free will and a surrender to destiny. Both songs describe prisoners of love, and if you simply saw the lyrics without hearing the music, you'd think they were a psychotherapist's notes from a session with a deeply paranoid young woman trapped in a sadomasochistic relationship. Yet with "Chains," sung by the Cookies, girls were primed for danc-ing from the very beginning by the hand clapping, snare drums, and saxophones, so that the music worked in stark contrast to the lyrics, which claimed that the girl couldn't break free from her chains of love. Then, in a break from the chorus, the lead singer acknowledged, "I wanna tell you pretty baby/Your lips look sweet/I'd like to kiss them/But I can't break away from all of these chains." At least two personas emerge here, coexisting in the same teenager. One is the girl who loves the bittersweet condition of being hopelessly consumed by love. The other is the girl who, despite her chains, has a roving and appreciative eye for other boys. The conflict between the sense of entrapment in the lyrics and the utter liberation of the beat is inescapable. The tension is too delicious for words.

It was the same for one of the greatest songs ever recorded, "Nowhere to Run." The opening layers of drums, horns, and tambourines propelled us out onto the dance floor—I mean, you couldn't not dance to this song. While we were gyrating and bouncing around to a single about a no-good boy who promised nothing but heartache yet had us in his sadistic grip, we were as happy as we could be. The best part was the double entendre lyrics in the middle, which we belted out with almost primal intensity. "How can I fight a love that shouldn't be?/When it's so deep—so deep—it's deep inside of me/My love reaches so high I can't get over it/So wide, I can't get around it, no." In the face of our entrapment, Martha Reeves made us sweat, and celebrated the capacity of girls to love like women. She also articulated a sophisticated knowingness about how sexual desire overtakes common sense every time, even in girls. In a very different kind of song, the effervescent "I Can't Stay Mad at You," Skeeter Davis told her boyfriend that he could treat her like dirt, make her cry, virtually grind her heart under the heel of his boot, and she'd still love him anyway, and all this between a string of foot-tapping, butt-bouncing shoobie doobie do bops. So even in songs seemingly about female victimization and helplessness, the beat and euphoria of the music put the lie to the lyrics by getting the girl out on the dance floor, moving on her own, doing what she liked, displaying herself sexually, and generally getting ready for bigger and better things. Dancing to this music together created a powerful sense of unity, of commonality of spirit, since we were all feeling, with our minds and our bodies, the same enhanced emotions at the same moment.

While a few girl groups and individual singers were white—the Angels, the Shangri-Las, Dusty Springfield—most successful girl groups were black. Unlike the voices of Patti Page or Doris Day, which seemed as innocent of sexual or emotional angst as a

Chatty Cathy doll, the vibrating voices of black teenagers, often trained in the gospel traditions of their churches, suggested a perfect fusion of naivete and knowingness. And with the rise of the civil rights movement, which by 1962 and 1963 dominated the national news, black voices conveyed both a moral authority and a spirited hope for the future. These were the voices of exclusion, of hope for something better, of longing. They were not, like Annette or the Lennon Sisters, the voices of sexual repression, of social complacency, or of homogenized commercialism.

From the Jazz Age to rap music, African American culture has always kicked white culture upside the head for being so pathologically repressed; one consequence, for black women, is that too often they have been stereotyped as more sexually active and responsive than their white-bread sisters. Because of these stereotypes, it was easier, more acceptable, to the music industry and no doubt to white culture at large that black girls, instead of white ones, be the first teens to give voice to girls' changing attitudes toward sex. But since the sexuality of black people has always been deeply threatening to white folks, black characters in popular culture also have been desexualized, the earth-mother mammy being a classic example. The black teens in girl groups, then, while they sounded orgiastic at times, had to look feminine, innocent, and as white as possible. Berry Gordy, the head of Motown, knew this instinctively, and made his girl groups take charm school lessons and learn how to get into and out of cars, carry their handbags, and match their shoes to their dresses. They were trapped, and in the glare of the spotlight, no less, between the old and new definitions of femininity. But under their crinolined skirts and satin cocktail dresses, they were also smuggling into middle-class America a taste of sexual liberation. So white girls like me owe a cultural debt to these black girls for straddling these contradictions, and for helping create a teen girl culture that said, "Let loose, break free, don't take no shit."

The Shirelles paved the way for the decade's most successful girl group, the Supremes, who had sixteen records in the national top ten between 1964 and 1969. But of utmost importance was the role Diana Ross played in making African American beauty enviable to white girls. As slim as a rail with those cavernous armpits, gorgeous smile, and enormous, perfectly made-up eyes, Diana Ross is the first black woman I remember desperately wanting to look like, even if some of her gowns were a bit too Vegas. I couldn't identify with her completely, not because she was black, but because when I was fourteen, she seemed so glamorous and sophisticated. Ross has taken a lot of heat in recent years as the selfish bitch who wanted all the fame and glory for herself, so it's easy to forget her importance as a cultural icon in the 1960s. But the Supremes—who seemed to be both girls and women, sexy yet respectable, and a blend of black and white culture—made it perfectly normal for white girls to idolize and want to emulate their black sisters.

Another striking trend that grew out of the girl group revolution was the proliferation of the male falsetto. From Maurice Williams in "Stay" to Lou Christie in "Two Faces Have I" to Roy Orbison in "Crying" and Randy and the Rainbows in "Denise" (ooo-be-ooo), and most notably with the Four Seasons and the Beach Boys, boys sang in high-pitched soprano ranges more suited for female than for male sing-along. What this meant was that girls belting out lyrics in the kitchen, in the car, or while watching *American Bandstand* had the opportunity to assume *male* roles, male subjective stances as they sang, even though they were singing in a female register.

This was nothing less than musical cross-dressing. While the male falsettos sang of their earnest love for their girls, about how those girls got them through the trials and tribulations of parental disputes, loneliness, drag-car racing ("Don't Worry Baby"), or being from the wrong side of the tracks, girls could fantasize about boys being humanized, made more nurturing, compassionate, and sensitive through their relationships with girls. This is an enduring fantasy, and one responsible for the staggeringly high sales of romance novels in America. It was a narcissistic fantasy that the girl was at the center of someone's universe, that she did make a difference in that universe, and that that difference was positive. This practice of assuming male voices later enabled girls to slip in and out of male points of view, sometimes giving girls a temporary taste of power. Several years later, in a song much maligned by feminists, "Under My Thumb," girls could and did sing not as the one under the thumb but as the one holding the thumb down.

While girl group music celebrated love, marriage, female masochism, and passivity, it also urged girls to make the first move, to rebel against their parents and middle-class conventions, and to dump boys who didn't treat them right. Most of all, girl group music—precisely because these were groups, not just individual singers—insisted that it was critically important for girls to band together, talking about men, singing about men, trying to figure them out.

What we have here is a pop culture harbinger in which girl groups, however innocent and commercial, anticipate women's groups, and girl talk anticipates a future kind of women's talk. The consciousness-raising groups of the late sixties and early seventies came naturally to many young women because we'd had a lot of practice. We'd been talking about boys, about loving them and hating them, about how good they often made us feel and how bad they often treated us, for ten years. The Shirelles mattered because they captured so well our confusion in the face of changing sexual mores. And as the confusion of real life intersected with the contradictions in popular culture, girls were prepared to start wondering, sooner or later, why sexual freedoms didn't lead to other freedoms as well.

Girl group music gave us an unprecedented opportunity to try on different, often conflicting, personas. For it wasn't just that we could be, as we sang along first with the Dixie Cups and then the Shangri-Las, traditional passive girls one minute and more active, rebellious, even somewhat prefeminist girls the next. Contradiction was embedded in almost all the stances a girl tried on, and some version, no matter how thwarted, of prefeminism, constituted many of them. We couldn't sustain this tension forever, especially when one voice said, "Hey, hon, you're equal" and the other voice said, "Oh no, you're not."

The Shirelles and the other girl groups mattered because they helped cultivate inside us a desire to rebel. The main purpose of pop music is to make us feel a kind of euphoria that convinces us that we can transcend the shackles of conventional life and rise above the hordes of others who do get trapped. It is the euphoria of commercialism, designed to get us to buy. But this music did more than that; it generated another kind of euphoria as well. For when tens of millions of young girls started feeling, at the same time, that they, as a generation, would not be trapped, there was planted the tiniest seed of a social movement.

Few symbols more dramatically capture the way young women in the early 1960s were pinioned between entrapment and freedom than one of the most bizarre icons of the period, the go-go girl dancing in a cage. While African American performers like the Dixie Cups or Mary Wells sang on *Shindig* or *Hullabaloo*, white girls in white go-go boots pranced and shimmied in their cages in the background. Autonomous yet objectified, free to dance by herself on her own terms yet highly choreographed in her little prison, seemingly indifferent to others yet trapped in a voyeuristic gaze, the go-go girl seems, in retrospect, one of the sicker, yet more apt, metaphors for the teen female condition during this era. It's not surprising that when four irreverent, androgynous, and irresistible young men came over from England and incited a collective jailbreak, millions of these teens took them up on it. For we had begun to see some new kinds of girls in the mass media—some perky, some bohemian, some androgynous—who convinced us that a little anarchy was exactly what we, and American gender roles, needed.

QUESTIONS

---

1. What specific messages were embedded in the "girl group" music? What were some of the contradictions in these messages? How are these messages related to race? Why does the author consider this music revolutionary?

2. What role does identification play in the interpretation and popularity of this type of music? How did the music help create cultural unity or cohesion? What is the cultural significance of singing in groups?

3. How is the "girl group" music related to the new dances of the 1960s? How did technological changes like the transistor radio contribute to the significance of this type of music?

4. Why did the Shirelles matter? How was this type of music related to the social movements of the time? Was it a form of pre-feminism?